ROBERT DONINGTON
String Playing in Baroque Music

ROBERT DONINGTON
String Playing in Baroque Music

with recorded illustrations by
YEHUDI MENUHIN
GEORGE MALCOLM
ROBERT DONINGTON

Charles Scribner's Sons

New York

This book is accompanied by a stereo record
FR 105, on which the illustrations referred to in the
text are recorded by Yehudi Menuhin,
George Malcolm and Robert Donington

Music

Contents

Introduction

This book offers a practical demonstration of the style and technique of string playing which we believe makes for the best effect, under ordinary modern conditions of performance, in baroque music. Yehudi Menuhin and I found ourselves arriving, from different directions, at very much the same view of the case. There is the musicology of it; and there is the musicianly performance. As a musicologist, I feel acutely the uselessness of any musicology on the subject which does not end up as a beautiful string line, beautifully phrased and moulded. As a violinist, Menuhin is equally aware of the need to know how that line was originally meant to be shaped, with what colourings of the tone, with what articulation of the notes, and everything else which goes to a stylish performance fitted lovingly to the actual music. If this link between musicianly eloquence and musicological knowledge is not firmly enough connected up, then something will be lacking of that fire and that rightness of style, both of which have to be combined if a proper baroque performance is to result.

Unless the strings are getting more or less the right sonority and the right articulation, nothing else can be got to sound quite right where they are involved; and it is here that we can perhaps do most to improve the ordinary run of our baroque performances. It is not simply a matter of broad conception, but of technical detail. Bow strokes, fingerings, vibrato: it is of such technical elements as these that style is made. How were they practised then? How can they be fused into a spontaneous musical experience now? We need the historical information, and we need the skill and insight to make great music of it and not merely a careful reproduction, which is only too likely to be not a living reproduction at all but a deadly caricature.

When we found George Malcolm in agreement with us, and ready to take an active part, we felt we had a team which could attempt a suitable combination of the two approaches. We had at Faber Music a colleague equally resourceful and enthusiastic, Julian Elloway. The text of the book is my responsibility. It is a blend of historical facts as to how they did it then, with practical suggestions as to how we may wish to do it now. It is crucial to my argument that there is not only one acceptable way of doing it now; nor was there, I think, even at the time. There is and always was a wide range of options, through which the personality of the performer can rightly be expressed. There are also, however, outer boundaries to any style, outside which it is inevitable to be wrong and possible to be very wrong indeed. My explanatory text tries to show whereabouts the boundaries lie, and how to keep within them by using appropriate techniques of fiddling.

The recorded illustrations are the test of the argument and the essence of the demonstration. They are not put forward as infallibly correct; and still less is my text put forward as infallibly correct. How can any of us be all that sure of what went on centuries ago and has been long forgotten or much distorted on the way down? But there is so much more to an authentic performance than mere literal correctness. Above all, there is the line, and the phrasing which makes sense within the line. There is the unfaltering flow of sound, rising and falling in great arches but never flagging without musical intention. There are the timely breaks and stretchings which make intelligible patterns within the line. There is the glow and sparkle of glorious string tone. All this was as much appreciated in baroque times as in our own, and there can be no authenticity without it. This is what the recordings chiefly demonstrate, in addition to illustrating many of the details of technique discussed in my written text. It is the soaring intensity of Menuhin's line, and the unfailing inventiveness of Malcolm's realizations, which impress me the most. There is plenty of room for disagreement over this option or that; for it is part of the baroque spirit that there should be options. But here is a working sample of one essentially authentic style of baroque fiddling for modern times, and I do not mind saying that I think it is worth more than all my thoughtful words of advice put together. So be it; the book always was intended to be a package deal.

King's College
University of London   ROBERT DONINGTON
October 1974

PART ONE
The Approach

CHAPTER I

Baroque Fiddling for Modern Fiddlers

1 Baroque fiddling needs transparency and crispness

String-playing is the start of a good performance in the greater part of baroque music. Excepting for keyboard solos, there is not very much baroque music in which the strings do not take a share, and it is often a predominant share. The baroque orchestra, though varied and colourful, is built around the standard body of strings. Sonatas for solo violin with continuo accompaniment and, still more, trio sonatas for two violins with continuo accompaniment are among the most typical of baroque forms.

There is something in the way baroque music is composed which requires that the sound of string instruments should be transparent. Voices and wind instruments are subject to the same requirement; but voice-production is an art in itself, with Italian bel canto as its foundation, while wind playing, though not without its special problems for baroque performance, does not usually raise a problem in this particular matter of transparent sounds. But for baroque fiddling, it is the problem of problems.

There is a second requirement, connected with the first. This is a clean cutting edge. If the moment of attack is very massive, it is like using a blunt implement where a razor sharpness would do a better job. If the moment of attack is very smooth in the wrong places, it produces a pattern too soft for clearness. Here, also, voices and wind instruments need, just as much, this crispness of attack. Nevertheless, it is remarkable how quickly a concerted baroque performance begins to fall into shape as soon as the sound and attack of any string instruments involved have been brought into proper baroque style.

Proper baroque style includes a very complete and varied range of colourings (left-hand as well as right-hand) and almost every bow stroke of which string instruments are capable. But there are a few exceptions. Moreover, the choice of colouring and of bow stroke has always to be guided by the passage in question. There are many kinds of passage in baroque music, and many styles of fiddling with which to suit them. A bad choice for whatever reason will blur the passage and reduce its radiance, whereas a good choice will focus it and let its radiance glow out in full baroque glory. It is very important to know what goes with what.

Although there are so many kinds of baroque passages, and so many good styles of fiddling to go with them, some quality remains in common among them all. That quality very largely depends upon what has just been described: a transparent sonority; and a crisp articulation.

2 Baroque fiddling in modern circumstances

We may take for our starting point, then, the necessity for transparent sonority and crisp articulation in baroque fiddling.

These qualities are indispensable; but there are more ways than one of going after them. The most radical way is by reconstructing so far as we can the actual sounds of baroque fiddling. This was pioneered over half a century ago by Arnold Dolmetsch, and has now been taken up again on a wider scale, with results which at best (for example with Eduard Melkus) are most impressive and enjoyable. A less radical way is not to aim at the actual sounds of baroque fiddling, but only at sounds which, without being quite the baroque sounds, are compatible with the baroque style. This, too, seems to me perfectly acceptable.

Music is always tailored more or less to its original conditions of performance, and will not stand too much of a bad fit later on. But it is we who have to wear the clothes, and a certain working compromise with history need not be unsuccessful artistically. A modern fiddler using his ordinary instrument and bow cannot sound like a baroque fiddler; but he can use enough of the baroque technique to sound within the baroque style. It is also possible to sound out of style when using instruments of baroque character; for it is always the player rather than the implement that matters most. We may start by considering the character of the baroque implements, since they have much to teach us about performance. We can then decide better how much importance to attach to using them.

CHAPTER II

The Baroque Violin

1 Differences in the baroque instrument

The original condition of the baroque violin family and its fittings is that condition in which Stradivarius and the other master-craftsmen of that great age of violin-making made and fitted their instruments. We have moderate information as to what that condition was, because a small number of their instruments actually survive unaltered, and indeed so far as can be ascertained unopened.

Violins were still being made and fitted more or less to the baroque condition during the second half of the eighteenth century, that is to say during the classical period. A violin made during this period was recently found at Vienna in an unchanged condition: when used for a Mozart violin sonata, with a grand piano (fortepiano) of that period and style, it gave a very new and remarkable idea of the nature of this music, both for texture and for balance.

In the course of the nineteenth century, however, the fashionable ideals of sonority and articulation altered greatly, and with them the condition of the violin and its fittings. With the extremely rare exceptions mentioned above, all the instruments by the baroque master-craftsmen which now survive have been opened and altered to the modern condition normal at the present time. It is perfectly possible to open and restore them again to their original baroque condition. But not only is this a fairly drastic operation: it has the disadvantage of unfitting the instrument for its more modern uses.

The actual body of the violin has not been changed, however, and is not to be improved upon from its best specimens, though it has in some ways become more scientifically understood. But the bass-bar, which is a very important member of the structure, has been enlarged and strengthened for greater loudness, yielding more massive but less free vibrations. There has probably been some gain in power, some loss in transparent colouring, resulting from this heavier bass-bar. Our modern sound-post may also be a little stouter than the baroque average.

The angle at which the neck is set to the body has been increased, and the bridge raised to correspond; the neck itself has been lengthened by comparison with the baroque average, while our strings are also thicker (or covered, which has the same effect). Longer, heavier strings, crossing the bridge at a steeper angle, necessitate greater tension for the same pitch; and this, too, tends to more opaque power and less transparent colouring.

It is commonly stated that standard baroque pitch was a semitone lower than our customary $a' = 440$ (c.p.s.: vibration cycles per second). This statement is not strictly correct: there was no standard baroque pitch, but a great variety of different pitches, sometimes higher, sometimes lower, sometimes much the same as ours. However, it is true that the tension on a baroque violin was for several reasons lower, giving less massiveness but more freedom to the resulting vibrations. (Our recordings are at $a' = 440$.)

All the strings on the early baroque violin were of plain, uncovered gut, including the bottom string, which has then to be rather too thick and too slack for a very strong sound; and that is possibly why early baroque violin parts seldom go down on to the G string. Gimping (gut strings overspun with fine copper or silver wire) was introduced probably around the middle of the seventeenth century, after which covered bottom strings (violin G, viola C, cello G and C) became normal, with very satisfactory results. But still the lower tension favoured sounds less massive and neutral, more free and colourful, than is the modern fashion.

Fifty years ago, the normal stringing of the violin was a fine steel top E, a gut A and D, and a silver-covered gut bottom G. The two lower strings of the viola and the cello might be covered; the two upper strings, plain gut. The subsequent trend was towards further covered strings: first an aluminium-covered D on the violin, later a covered A and even E (sometimes with a core of steel wire). All four covered strings are now usual (or a steel wire E may be used); there are advantages in uniformity, stability and reliability, but the sound of the violin family has been considerably changed in consequence, and I think for the worse.

2 The mute

The mute is a device for loading the bridge with added weight and stiffness, giving greater resistance to vibration: the pitch is not altered, but the sound is partially muffled, yielding a tone of veiled and bodiless quality which in the romantic period was quite frequently exploited for its somewhat mysterious and supposedly poetical effect.

Mutes were known and used throughout the baroque period. There is a description in Mersenne (*Harmonie Universelle*, Paris, 1636–7, II, iv, 189); and

Jean-Jacques Rousseau (*Dictionnaire*, Paris, 1768, 'Sourdine') praised the Italians for making a special effect of them, and disparaged the French for despising them (but Rousseau was always looking for a stick to beat French music with). Quantz (*Essay*, Berlin, 1752, XVI, 28) mentioned 'an arioso which is played piano or with mutes'.

Thus there is nothing unhistorical in using the mute for baroque music which may be thought to be artistically suited by it, such as the slow movement of a Vivaldi concerto or the like. But even so, muted violins make a very impoverished sound by comparison with unmuted violins played as softly; and any sound so covered and so unclear is contrary to the transparent sonority and serene spirit characteristic of baroque music in general.

3 Differences in the baroque bow

The modern bow as used, in different weights and stiffnesses, on all members of the violin family, resembles the baroque bow in principle but not in design. There is a wooden stick of suitable resilience, with horse-hair (or a more or less satisfactory modern substitute) stretched from one end to the other, the friction of which across the strings sets them into cyclic vibration, thus exciting the tone which the body amplifies and transmits to the surrounding air.

But on the one hand, the baroque bow has a simple *outward* curvature, increased by the heightened tension as the bow is screwed up or otherwise tightened before playing; and also increased by the heightened tension as the bow is pressed on the string in course of playing.

The degree of curvature varies considerably, but in most specimens, and perhaps in all the best ones, it is so slight that even when the bow is screwed up to playing tension, the stick remains almost straight though very taut. If it is not very taut, it has probably not been screwed up nearly tight enough: a mistake into which an unaccustomed modern player may easily fall, since the modern bow to which he is accustomed is not, and must not be, screwed up so tight.

The length of the baroque bow also varies, from a delicate little implement some eighteen inches long (delightful in quick dances or Corelli allegros but frustrating in adagio) to an outsize implement longer than the modern bow by several inches (possibly welcome in the long, slow notes of an adagio; undoubtedly cumbersome in allegro unless the hold is shifted a few inches away from the frog, thus in effect shortening the bow, as we sometimes see done in contemporary pictures). But most specimens, and in general the best, are about two or three inches shorter than the modern length (this needs getting used to, but is otherwise no problem, being altogether suitable for baroque purposes). The breadth of the hairs is a little less.

And on the other hand, the modern bow has a logarithmic *inward* curvature, which is not diminished so much by the heightened tension when the bow is screwed up before playing, or by the pressure of the hair against the string in course of playing, the incurved stick maintaining its resistance like a cantilever. Nevertheless, it cannot be pressed too hard, at the middle of the bow, without the small clearance there between wood and hair closing up, and the wood scraping on the strings, especially in chords. The old bow has the advantage here.

The degree of the curvature and the length of the stick are more or less standardized in modern bows. The transition from an outcurved bow to an incurved bow occurred quite gradually during the eighteenth century. There are many late-baroque specimens which show a decidedly inward curvature when not screwed up to playing tension, and a straight or almost straight stick when screwed up: some of them play quite well, but not so well either as a typically outcurved baroque bow, or as a fully developed, incurved modern bow.

The full development of this transitional type into the modern type was the great achievement of the Tourte family, and especially of François Tourte, the most famous bow-maker of any period: and with reason; for he seems to have perfected the logarithmic curve which gives to the modern bow its remarkable combination of strength and resilience, constant under a wide range of playing pressures.

4 Differences in holding the instrument

The chin-rest is a fairly modern invention, not known to baroque fiddlers.

The baroque violin and viola were held in two main ways. One hold, quite commonly seen in pictures, was against the chest. Dance fiddlers often used it, and it is perfectly comfortable except that shifts are rather hard to manage: shifting up is easy enough, with the fiddle pressed against the chest; shifting down needs skill in order not to let the fiddle drop. Yet even serious fiddlers could use this hold without hampering themselves, since we read in Geminiani's famous method, *The Art of Playing on the Violin* (London, 1751, p. [2]) that 'the Head of the Violin must be nearly Horizontal with that Part which rests against the Breast, that the Hand may be shifted with Facility and without any Danger of dropping the Instrument'. He takes us up to the seventh position on all four strings.

The other baroque hold, also very commonly seen in pictures, was under the chin. The chin or the cheek may rest against the table, on either side of the tailpiece (as the perspiration marks on many old violins confirm). This is essentially the modern hold, and has no disadvantages. On the contrary, it is altogether to be recommended for baroque as for other music.

The baroque cello was held between the calves of the legs, without an end-pin, which was not always used even in the nineteenth century. But the comfort and security of an end-pin make it generally advantageous.

5 Differences in holding the bow

Baroque violinists and viola players held the bow in two main ways: one quite different from the modern way; the other either the same, or not very different.

(i) The quite different baroque way of holding the bow was by setting the thumb not, as we do, under the stick, but under the hair: this was the French grip, used by many French violinists or others playing (particularly in South Germany) with a French technique. It gives a good if rather unsubtle hold; but it does not, as has been incorrectly stated in modern times, enable the player to adjust the tension of the hair, so as to make chords easy, by varying the pressure of his thumb. (If in doubt, try it for yourself, but over the carpet, because you are probably going to drop the bow in course of the experiment.)

There never was any type of baroque bow with which this alleged thumb-adjustment was possible. The modern Vega bow can do it by means of a trigger; but this, though called the 'Bach bow', has nothing to do with Bach or with baroque music, and the misunderstanding on which it was designed has now been abandoned by all reputable scholars.

(ii) The not so different baroque way of holding the bow varied from a grip identical with a modern grip (and looking in some contemporary pictures exactly like the grip taught by Carl Flesch when I attended his classes) to the same grip but a few inches up the stick away from the frog. Both of the holds are equally authentic.

We always, in our modern technique, grip the bow at the frog, so as to have the full length of it at our disposal (and there are times when we would be glad enough to have a little more). Many baroque fiddlers evidently did the same; and this is very strongly my own recommendation. But some of them seem to have preferred a different balance, gained by moving the grip up the stick, as described in some methods and shown in some pictures. Leopold Mozart, in his excellent *Violinschule* (Augsburg, 1756), has pictures showing both a modern-style grip at the frog, as we hold the bow, and the same grip a few inches up the stick, as they sometimes held it, perhaps chiefly in quick movements so as to get the delicacy, in effect, of a shorter bow.

Baroque cellists held the bow in two main ways: one with the hand under the bow, in the ordinary manner of the viol; the other (less common) with the hand over the bow, in the normal modern grip; but in both holds, sometimes (as with the violinists) a few inches along the stick away from the frog. I strongly recommend the grip at the nut, as I also do for bowing on the viols. It can be done no less delicately, with skill; and it also allows for the full robustness so often required in baroque music.

6 How important are the differences in the instrument?

These historical differences are all of the greatest interest to modern performers who are concerned with reconstituting as far as possible the original sounds of baroque music.

Modern performers who are more concerned to bring baroque music forward into our own times than to pursue it back into its original conditions will be interested rather to ask how far these historical differences affect the artistic possibilities; and to this question we shall turn in the following chapter.

CHAPTER III

Departing from the Baroque Violin

1 The modern violin acceptable for baroque music

The violin when restored to its baroque condition (lighter bass-bar and sound-post, shorter neck set straighter to the body, lower bridge giving a shallower angle to the strings, shorter, slacker strings of uncovered gut except for the silver-covered gut bottom G) sounds less assertive, less massive, less of a general-purpose instrument; more colourful, more edgy, more pungent, more of a specialized and individual instrument; less uniform across the different strings; more naturally transparent.

The modern violin sounds more powerful, more smooth and more uniform. It has a less pungently stringy individuality. It is not so naturally transparent, nor so naturally disposed to blend in, though it can be controlled in these respects by the right technique. We might put it that the modern violin is a less specialized instrument than the baroque violin, and by the same argument, more versatile.

2 Whether to use a baroque violin

Thus a player specializing in baroque music is well served by a baroque violin under any circumstances not requiring (as, for example, an unusually big hall may require) the largest volume of sound. But a player ranging widely through the literatures of his instrument, as most players do, would not be well served by a baroque violin unless he is in a position to keep it as a second instrument in addition to one in ordinary modern condition.

If he decides to do this, it is now possible to buy an ordinary, decent old violin which has been opened up and put into baroque condition; or a new violin made to a baroque specification. He would still find some difficulty in changing over from one violin to the other during the actual progress of a recital, since they have of course quite a different feel. But he should be able to get a baroque sound.

On the other hand, an ordinary modern violinist, using a violin in ordinary modern condition, though he cannot get a baroque sound, can get a baroque style. Many of us find the quieter, sharper sounds of a baroque violin quite hauntingly beautiful and appropriate; but the modern violin has its own poetic intensity and vibrant power. It is, of course, what we are all used to, and is, perhaps, what the majority are always likely to prefer. Since most though not all of our readers will certainly be playing their baroque music on a violin in ordinary condition, it is important to know that this can be done, if not with full historical validity, nevertheless with full artistic validity. It can.

3 The colourful sound of uncovered gut strings

To have the internal fittings, bridge and neck of a violin reconstructed to baroque design is a drastic undertaking; but there is one possible compromise which goes some way in the baroque direction without involving any structural alterations. This is to string a violin (otherwise in modern condition) with uncovered gut strings, except that it is probably best to retain the normal silver-covered gut bottom G (itself in use by the middle of the baroque period).

The difference in the colouring and texture of the sound resulting from uncovered gut on the top three strings is quite audible and extremely enjoyable. The colouring is that much more pungent; the texture is that much more edgy. The tone is a little quieter; but this is advantageous rather than otherwise for baroque music in most ordinary acoustic circumstances. By no means every player today is going to like this return to gut stringing for baroque purposes. The experiment is very easy to make, however, and it is an experience which the enterprising reader may well wish to put to the test.

Gut stringing (apart from the covered bottom G) was the original condition not only in baroque music, but also in classical and romantic music. Joachim and Sarasate would still have been using gut E, A and D strings, and the wonderful purity and radiance of the sound can still be heard on their surviving recordings (for example, Joachim's fine Bach playing on G and T No. 047903, recorded in 1903; or Sarasate's own virtuoso *Capriccio basque* on Black G and T No. 37929, recorded in 1904).

The generation of Kreisler introduced the steel wire E, which gives a silvery beauty of tone in no way inappropriate to baroque style; but it has not the raw, rich and edgy pungency of a gut E. There is always some risk of a gut E string breaking in the course of a concert: a mishap which a concerto soloist used to deal with by instantly changing fiddles with the leader of the orchestra. There is virtually no risk of this with a gut A or a gut D. The sound of the gut E, A and D is certainly more baroque than that of steel or covered strings, and somewhat more characterful individually, though it is not so uniform over the whole of the fiddle, nor can it be drawn out quite so powerfully. A steel E is perfectly acceptable, and a silver-covered G is no doubt preferable, on a violin used for baroque music; while for any music until, perhaps, Bartók or Hindemith, there is great charm in this traditional stringing with at least the two middle strings of gut, and if one is brave enough, the top string also. Yehudi Menuhin told me that he has played Elgar's Violin Concerto quite recently with gut strings, and enjoyed the extraordinary sweetness and clarity of the sounds they gave him, though these sounds were not of the biggest.

Nevertheless, the stronger, smoother and more uniform quality of covered strings is the normal modern preference, and most violinists using this book will be stringing the instrument in the modern way. To change strings for the baroque pieces in course of a mixed recital would of course be disastrous; and even to change strings for a completely baroque recital would unsettle the tuning of the whole instrument unless it could be done a day or two beforehand. Once again, then, gut stringing is chiefly feasible for specialists whose violin can be kept regularly strung with gut; or for those in a position to own two good violins, one kept to gut stringing and the other to modern stringing.

Covered strings lack that exquisitely stringy glitter which only gut strings possess. But since gut strings are a little less reliable for intonation and (at least the E) for durability, as well as a little less capable of the loudest volume, the advantages are not all on one side. The core of a covered string should in any case be of gut rather than of metal. The sound of metal wound on metal is very perceptibly—well, should we say metallic; the sound of metal wound on gut has also, perhaps, a hint of this metallic quality. A covered E of any material is best avoided; and so, in my opinion, are plastic strings, in spite of their slightly superior reliability and stability, since they never quite deceive the ear. For sheer delight of sound, I must admit to an old-fashioned preference for gut. But it is perfectly possible to get the requisite transparency and incisiveness of sound, though in somewhat altered quality, when using a steel E string, and even when using covered (metal on gut) A, D and G strings, in baroque music.

4 Modern pitch normally acceptable for baroque music

There is no necessary artistic advantage, and no historical advantage at all, in habitually tuning down to a semitone below our standard modern pitch of $a' = 440$. Only for the Viennese classics is this lower pitch established as of some historical consequence, and as of some solid artistic advantage (for example, to the sopranos in the Ninth Symphony or the *Missa Solemnis* of Beethoven).

Our $a' = 440$ may be a little higher than is ideal, but it was at long last internationally agreed upon, and should be vigorously defended against current pressure *upwards*, if only because of the immense practical benefit of having a stable pitch everywhere. There is no general need to tune lower for baroque music, except where old woodwind instruments are being used which happen to require it. There may also be special circumstances, such as frail antique instruments which would not withstand the pressure of being tuned up to $a' = 440$. Most instruments will tolerate a small margin of different pitch; but few can be *altered* in pitch without becoming temporarily unsettled. A stable pitch wherever you go is the chief reason for staying generally with $a' = 440$.

5 Chin-rest and end-pin acceptable conveniences

The chin-rest, though unhistorical for baroque music, has little acoustic consequence, and the same is true of the cellist's or gambist's end-pin. There is therefore no artistic advantage in dispensing with the comfort of either of these two modern conveniences; and perhaps only the more thorough-going specialists will wish to do so. Most violinists have a type and height of chin-rest which suits them best, and cellists a length of end-pin. It will normally be wisest to keep them as usual, perhaps even for baroque specialists, and certainly for players with a general repertoire.

6 The modern bow tolerable for baroque music

Whereas the ordinary modern violin can be perfectly acceptable in baroque music, the ordinary modern bow is somewhat less acceptable, since it cannot do an absolutely satisfactory job for baroque purposes. Not only is it quite possible to hear the difference; this difference is frequently disadvantageous from the artistic as well as from the historical point of view.

The changes in the instrument chiefly influence the sonority. That difference can also be heard; but since either kind of sonority can be made suitably transparent, the artistic purpose can still be very well served either way. The changes in the bow chiefly influence the articulation. There is a certain kind of incisiveness without hardness which is eminently well suited to baroque music, and which the baroque bow does effortlessly as well as excellently, but which the modern bow cannot quite do either so effortlessly or so excellently.

The modern bow, properly handled, can nevertheless make a very close approach to the requisite baroque articulation. It is, therefore, a very tolerable though not an ideal implement for baroque purposes. Most modern violinists are likely to be using modern bows, as usual; and there is perhaps some advantage in using the same, familiar bow for all kinds of music. For it must always be remembered that it is not really the implement which gets the style right. It is the player. It is always more important to have a baroque sound in your head than a baroque instrument or even a baroque bow in your hands. That is the belief on which this book is based.

7 Whether to use a baroque bow

On the other hand, much that is more difficult with the modern bow, and not possible to achieve in full, can be done easily and fully with the baroque bow. It is therefore worth considering whether to buy a baroque bow and to keep it in the violin case for use whenever baroque music is being performed. It is a wonderful experience to play with a really good baroque bow, which positively helps the player towards getting a baroque sonority and still more a baroque articulation. The implement does not do the job. But it makes the job decidedly easier to do.

It must be a good bow. It must have a good stick: laterally straight, strong, in nice balance and of the right stiffness and elasticity. A genuine antique with a weak or a crooked stick is useless for serious playing purposes, however attractive and interesting it may look in a glass case. Good antique bows come up occasionally in the sale-room, at a price; but much more rarely than unsatisfactory ones.

It is now possible to buy reproduction baroque bows from a number of makers. The best of these play very well indeed, but subject to the same conditions. The stick must be laterally straight, strong, well balanced and of the right stiffness and elasticity.

One may well be thankful to buy a good antique bow of whatever length; but, old or new, the best length is no more than one or two or at most three inches shorter than the modern standard.

8 The modern bow grip excellent for baroque music

Any good and normal bow grip as taught in modern times is appropriate for baroque fiddling. Most or all of these bow grips are clearly to be seen in contemporary baroque pictures, as well as other variants, such as the grip a few inches up the stick from the nut, with which it is certainly instructive to experiment. But a player who has a good modern bow grip of his own will probably do best to stay with it for baroque purposes.

9 The essential quality of baroque fiddling

The situation so far outlined may be summarized as follows. It is not the instrument, and it is not the bow, which is going to make the crucial difference. It is the player: his understanding of the style; his use of the appropriate techniques; his trained musicianship.

We are the children of our times, and our trained musicianship is conditioned by our times. We can only experience music in the present tense, making over for ourselves whatever its past may have to offer us. If we prefer baroque sounds, it is we who have to pour conviction into them. If we prefer modern implements, it is we who have to make them sound suitable for the baroque purpose. Not our historical fidelity but our artistic integrity is the real test, and our history will only ring true when our artistry has absorbed it.

But if fidelity to the past is not perhaps a particularly important end, it can be a very important means. There are artistic boundaries to every style, which are built into the music and do not change with the passing of the years. There is ample room inside them for most temperaments, but only hollow display outside. If there is anything certain about interpretation it is that there is no one certain interpretation. But there are outer limits, and we may next consider what these are for baroque fiddling, bearing in mind that it is not so much the literal baroque sounds as the essential quality of them which the ordinary modern fiddler will want to cultivate.

PART TWO
The Technique

CHAPTER IV

How Much Bow?

1 Right hand and left hand

The sound of a bowed instrument varies (apart from the actual instrument and its fitting up) through two distinct though connected causes: (i) right-hand technique, i.e. basically bow-strokes; and (ii) left-hand technique, i.e. basically finger-work.

    (i) Bow-strokes differ from one another in

        (a) speed (see p. 28);
        (b) pressure (see p. 28);
        (c) angle of hair (see p. 28);
        (d) distance from the bridge (see p. 28);
        (e) part of the bow (see p. 31f.);
        (f) joins and separations (see p. 43f.);
        (g) other nuances (see p. 54f.).

Of these factors, some mainly influence the sonority, and some the articulation, while all are concerned in that crucial dimension which we call *expression*. Pizzicato is also a branch of right-hand (and occasionally of left-hand) technique.

    (ii) Finger-work differs in

        (h) choice of fingerings (see p. 61);
        (i) choice of position (see p. 62);
        (j) strength of impact (see p. 65);
        (k) degree of portamento if any (see p. 65);
        (l) degree of vibrato (see p. 66).

Much of this is strictly more wrist work or arm work than finger work, but all of it has to do with left-hand colouring and nuancing. Open strings are one choice of fingering (no stopping finger) included in left-hand technique. Both sonority and articulation can be affected by left-hand technique, and as usual, expression is the overall objective.

2 A combination of factors

The sonority caused by a bow stroke results from a combination of factors, closely related to one another. Other things being equal:

(a) The greater the speed, the more the energy tends to go into high rather than low harmonics, and thus to yield a somewhat flute-like and insubstantial sonority. The less the speed, the more the energy tends to go into low rather than high harmonics, and to yield a somewhat stringier and solider sonority.

Moreover, the greater the speed, the louder the volume up to a certain point of diminishing returns, beyond which the hair cannot bite on the string firmly enough to impart full energy. The less the speed, the less the volume, down to a point at which there is not enough energy being generated to keep the string in continuous vibration, even if the bow hand could control a motion so excessively slow.

Moderate speeds are normal speeds: very great speeds and very small speeds of bow stroke are more or less special effects, valuable but only for their own special purposes, which are not characteristically baroque although they can occur.

(b) The greater the pressure, the greater the amplitude of vibration and the louder the volume, up to a point beyond which greater pressure crushes the vibrations rather than enlarging them, and gritty scratches occur. The less the pressure, the less the amplitude of vibration and the softer the volume, down to a point at which there is insufficient pressure to excite the lower vibrations continuously, and the tone vanishes in a whisper of high harmonics.

A wide range of pressures is normal; greater extremes are for special effects, of very restricted value in baroque music.

(c) The more tilted the angle of the hair to the string, the narrower the band of hair in contact at normal pressures, the less damping of the very high harmonics, but also the less ample exciting of the lowest harmonics, so that more colour but less solidity is yielded. The less tilted the angle of the hair to the string, the wider the band of hair in contact, the more damping of the very high harmonics (such as are produced by very short lengths of the string), but also the more ample exciting of the lower harmonics (especially the fundamental), so that less colour but more solidity is yielded.

(d) The closer to the bridge, the more massive the vibration and the stronger but less poetical the sound, up to a point of diminishing returns at which the lower harmonics are virtually eliminated, and that eerie, bottomless sound is yielded which the instruction *sul ponticello*, by the bridge, indicates. The further from the bridge, the less massive the vibration and the weaker but more poetical the sound, up to a point at which the lower harmonics are so weakened that the disembodied sound is yielded which the instruction *sul tasto*, by the fingerboard, indicates.

The actual distance of the bow from the bridge at which normal sounds are yielded is different for each string, and also for each length stopped on each string, but lies within quite a narrow margin in each instance. The greatest extremes are not appropriate to baroque music, of which the entire character would seem to be unsuited either to *sul ponticello* or to *sul tasto* effects. If exceptions do occur, they would have to be for special reasons.

3 A tone robust but not strenuous

In practice, other things never are equal. On the contrary, speed, pressure, angle of hair and distance from the bridge are factors whose success depends upon their subtle balance in combination.

When a bow stroke combines great speed, great pressure, somewhat flat hair, somewhat close to the bridge, the tone yielded is both robust and strenuous. A sound so violent and so opaque seems quite opposed to the spirit and technique of any baroque music.

Magnificent in Brahms, catastrophic in Bach, this very strenuous bow stroke should be avoided for all ordinary purposes (perhaps for all purposes) of baroque fiddling. It is not characteristic of baroque music to be strenuous. On the other hand, it is often characteristic of baroque music to be robust.

There is nothing either historical (as shown by the contemporary evidence) or artistic (as shown by the musical results) to support the idea that baroque music has to be scaled-down and essentially reticent. 'Draw an honest and manly tone from the violin', wrote Leopold Mozart (*Violinschule*, Augsburg, 1756, II, 5); even a beginner, he adds, should not be put off merely because 'the roughness of a strong bowing which has not yet been purified is harsh to the ear', for with growing skill, 'purity will be combined with strength of tone'.

How can we take the strenuousness out of such a bow stroke, while keeping the robustness? We can modify the combination of factors. We can slow down the speed of the bow, while retaining most of the pressure, and the somewhat flat hair somewhat close to the bridge. To use a phrase which every good string player understands, we can play more into the string.

To play into the string means to rely less on speed than on pressure for strength of sound. A fast bow gets volume as well as a firm bow; but the effect is different. The fast bow sounds more agitated, the firm bow sounds more stable; and while both these emotions and many others do find their place in baroque music, and do require their appropriate techniques, on the whole a certain controlled excitement is its most characteristic quality. Baroque robustness calls not for strenuous sounds but for focused sounds.

4 A tone colourful but not tenuous

It is not only in loud passages that we need what Leopold Mozart called 'an honest and manly tone from the violin'. He goes on (V, 12): 'we must manage the bow from loud to soft in such a way that a good, steady, singing, and as it were round, fat tone can always be heard'.

When a bow stroke combines great speed, little pressure, and somewhat tilted hair somewhat far from the bridge, the tone yielded is both colourful and tenuous. There are passages in baroque music which perhaps imply it and which certainly accept it. Thus it is not always out of place in baroque music.

Nevertheless, this kind of soft tone, produced by great speed and little pressure of the bow, is not the kind which Leopold Mozart recommended for general baroque use, when he called for a 'good, steady, singing, and as it were round, fat tone' both in loud and in soft playing. He did not mean that this round, fat tone should never be varied for any number of special purposes; on the contrary, he gives careful instructions to use high positions for poetic colourings and the like. But as a general-purpose standard of tone, soft as well as loud, he recommended the solider sounds of the violin. Not tenuous sounds, but (once again) focused sounds.

How can we take the tenuousness out of such a bow stroke, while keeping the softness? Again, by modifying the combination of factors. We can slow down the speed of the bow, while slightly increasing the pressure and retaining the somewhat tilted hair somewhat far from the bridge. In a soft passage, not less than in a loud passage, we can play more into the string.

5 Playing into the string

We have now arrived, therefore, at one general recommendation, which is not invariably applicable, and which has to be adapted with due discretion to each different context, but which will nevertheless be found remarkably helpful in a great variety of baroque situations. This is to slow down the bow and use less of it, compensating as necessary by greater pressure and by keeping the hair a little flatter and a little nearer to the bridge. It is this recommendation which is summarized in the familiar phrase which I use perhaps more than any other when taking rehearsals of baroque music having string instruments: play more into the string.

CHAPTER V

What Part of the Bow?

1 Choosing the best part of the bow

We now come to a combination of factors by which the bow stroke influences both sonority and, still more, articulation. This is (e): the part of the bow to be used for any stroke which does not take the whole of it.

A stroke taken at or near the bottom of the bow puts the greatest weight from the arm on to the string, and thus gets the greatest natural strength, especially on the down bow, which goes with gravity. A stroke taken at or near the top of the bow puts the least weight from the arm on to the string, and thus gets the least natural strength, especially on the up bow, which goes against gravity. A stroke taken at or near the middle of the bow puts an intermediate weight from the arm on to the string, and thus gets an intermediate natural strength, though greater (because of gravity) on the down bow than on the up bow.

On the other hand, the force of leverage is greater at the top of the bow than at the bottom of the bow; and this makes it possible for a skilful player to compensate by differences of muscular pressure for differences of weight. The actual strength of the sonority can thus be equalized; but the means used are not the same, and the difference in effect, however skilfully disguised, is not abolished. Certain parts of the bow have the advantage for certain effects, and a good player will always exploit this advantage so far as possible.

For example, the advantage of a *short stroke at the heel* of the bow is for massive energy and abruptness. The energy can be effectively maintained, but the abruptness somewhat lessened, by moving the stroke a little away from the heel, say to the mid-point of the lower half of the bow. But this stroke (especially when taken quite at the heel) is inherently too strenuous to have much if any value in baroque music except for certain special effects (e.g. to strike three-part chords on three strings held simultaneously, a rather rare situation). Tartini, in his famous letter of instruction to his pupil Signora Lombardini, written from Padua, 5 March 1760, urged her to practise strokes at all other parts of the bow, but did not even mention strokes at the heel.

The advantage of a *short stroke at the tip* of the bow is for sparkling brilliance and delicacy. The brilliance can be effectively maintained, but the delicacy somewhat lessened, by moving the stroke a little away from the tip, say to the mid-point of the upper half of the bow.

The advantage of a *short stroke at the middle* of the bow is for medium energy and great suppleness. Very little energy is lost, however, and even greater suppleness is gained, by moving this stroke slightly up the bow, so that it uses, not the part equally on either side of the mid-point of the bow, but the part immediately above the mid-point of the bow. We may call this the upper middle of the bow. Its value for baroque music can hardly be exaggerated. It is the best of all short strokes for countless baroque passages.

2 Where the part of the bow is an open choice

For a passage wholly or mainly in notes of equal value, we can generally choose that part of the bow which has the greatest natural advantage for the effect intended.

Suppose, in baroque music, that we have a passage of allegro, wholly or mainly in running or leaping eighth notes (quavers). These are quite short notes at that tempo. They could, as an extreme measure, be given full strokes of the bow; but the musical effect would be so hideously over-strenuous for baroque music that no good violinist is likely to attempt it. Even half-strokes of the bow might still be too strenuous, though this would depend on the context. There certainly are some baroque allegros which invite a bold display of energy. But there are many more which want to flow along quite easily, with plenty of concentrated vitality, but with no undue effort. They make their point not so much by weight as by sharpness. About a quarter of the length of the bow, pressed firmly but not harshly into the string, gives them all the strength they need in forte; the same stroke, but with lighter pressure, gives them all the lightness they need in piano. There is not enough natural energy for this at the tip of the bow. There is too much natural energy at the heel of the bow. There is exactly the right amount of natural energy in the upper middle of the bow.

There is no stroke more characteristic of baroque music than this quite strong but beautifully relaxed stroke, just a little higher up the bow than its midway point. It is not only in the main melodies but also in the bass parts that the upper middle of the bow so often gives the best choice of stroke, for bass parts in baroque music have also to be phrased and nuanced as the expressive melodies they generally are.

Many a baroque allegro or andante has a bass part running along, and at times leaping along, mostly in eighth notes: but these eighth notes do not have to be pounded out in equal strength; they can be varied continually in strength and length, like the notes of any other melodic line, and they will suport the harmony all the better if this is done. They are commonly taken at the heel; but that inclines them to be too massive for their proper subtlety, and not sufficiently supple. A great deal of the work which cellists and bass players commonly do at the heel, for baroque music, can be done better in the upper middle of the bow.

Quarter notes (crotchets) in a baroque allegro, although of twice the value, nevertheless may often be eased along in much the same firm but relaxed melodic line as eighth notes (quavers). Where this is so, the same choice of stroke in the upper middle of the bow may suit them best, although the stroke will be longer: about one-third of the length of the bow is quite likely to be sufficient.

In slow movements, a greater intensity of tone is usually required. Short notes may need proportionately a swifter, longer stroke, and long notes may need that tautly focused sound, a subtle combination of pressure and economy of bow, which fiddlers call *son filé*, drawn sound. Left-hand colouring will also be very important here: see Ch. X (p. 61) below.

Some notes, especially in slow movements, are so long that, even with all due economy of bow, a full stroke is not sufficient for them. Economy of bow must never be carried so far that the tone suffers, or even so far as to feel uncomfortable and constricting. Well before that point is reached, the direction of the bow must be changed, and a fresh stroke taken.

Provided this is done with the necessary skill, it can be quite imperceptible; and it should be done as often as required. To change bow smoothly is far better than taking the slightest risk of running out of bow. There may, in some cases, be the further gain of getting into a better part of the bow for an ensuing passage. Looking ahead in such a manner is, of course, a very substantial aspect of good bowing technique.

3 Where the part of the bow is not an open choice

For a passage not wholly or mainly in notes of equal value, but having different values (both plain and dotted) interspersed, we may not always be able to reach that part of the bow which has the greatest natural advantage for the effect intended, but may have to do the best we can with a somewhat awkward situation, without letting the hearer suspect any difficulty.

Consider, for example, the main subject of the fugue which is the last movement of Bach's Fourth Brandenburg Concerto (Music Ex. A).

MUSIC EXAMPLE A
J.S. Bach, 4th Brandenburg, 4th movt.

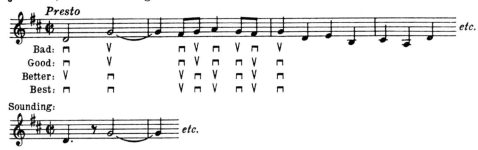

(i) It is possible to start this theme with a down bow (full length, since the note is moderately long and requires to be vigorous). The second note (also full bow, since the note is still longer) can then be taken with an up bow; but this means adjusting the bowing by two consecutive down bows in the second bar, unless the following passage is to be bowed with all the down beats on up bows.

(ii) It is also possible to start with an up bow; and this has the advantage that the subsequent bowings all work out very comfortably of their own accord. But with so strong a theme, we should probably prefer, other things being equal, to start down bow.

(iii) This, too, is possible, still more advantageously, if we take both the first two notes down bow. The first stroke, though still full length or nearly so, can be taken fast enough to leave time for getting back to the heel punctually for the second stroke; and the little silence which comes between them while this is done makes for excellent phrasing.

But now observe what falls out naturally for the shorter notes from these prior decisions concerning the longer notes.

(i) The first main alternative (starting down, up) brings the eighth notes (quavers) to the heel of the bow, which is not in itself the best part of the bow for them, though acceptable with good bow-control. Then if no adjustment is made by taking two consecutive down bows in the second bar, the quarter notes (crotchets) following will fall naturally at the middle of the bow, which is satisfactory, but the bowing will be upside down to the accents.

And if a subsidiary adjustment is made by taking two consecutive down bows in the second bar (which is what the French school of Lully and their German imitators such as Muffat would have done), the quarter notes following will fall naturally in the upper part of the bow, which is less strong but still quite satisfactory. The bow need not be lifted back between these two consecutive down bows, and no one need hear the difference, but the solution as a whole is not ideal.

34

(ii) The second main alternative (starting up, down) brings the eighth notes to the tip of the bow, which is the best part of the bow for them, since it is easiest there to control them with the requisite lightness. The quarter notes following will again fall naturally at the middle of the bow, where it is easiest to give them the requisite robustness without strenuousness; and on this choice, no adjustment is needed to bring them the right way up, with the down bows coinciding with the down beats.

(iii) The third alternative (starting down, down) has exactly the same results for the eighth notes and the quarter notes, and may well be preferred because it feels and sounds so good to start this powerful theme down bow, and because the silence of articulation enforced by lifting the bow back to the heel strengthens the phrasing in a way which may also seem good to many players; and certainly it comes across very clearly to the audience. That is a most important advantage. This is therefore the recommended bowing.

CHAPTER VI

Bowings on the String

1 Bowing techniques the result of the properties of the bow

The next factor to be considered in combination with those already considered as influencing sonority and articulation is (f): the joins and separations between bow strokes which give them character and adaptability.

The different manners of joining bow strokes, with a degree of separation ranging from least (legato) to most (staccato), depend upon exploiting the physical properties of the bow: its weight; its stiffness; its elasticity; its varying behaviour when different parts of it are in contact with the string.

Since these properties are not quite the same for the baroque bow and the modern bow, the effects produced are not quite the same either; but they are essentially the same. We use the same techniques, and we produce the same articulations, although the baroque bow makes them come out with a rather different character, more crisp than forceful, and more rounded than hard.

Some techniques are easier with the modern bow (e.g. spiccato), others are easier with the baroque bow (e.g. the sprung détaché to be described below). But there is no technique possible on the one bow which is not also possible on the other bow, with varying degrees of effectiveness and suitability.

2 The smoothest legato a necessity for baroque cantabile

The smoothest manner of joining one bow stroke to another is controlled by the slightest flexibility of the wrist and (as Carl Flesch used to teach it) of the fingers; and it can be so imperceptible that the effect is like a single bow stroke indefinitely prolonged. There is then no audible separation of the strokes at all, but an unbroken continuity. They are completely legato, 'bound'.

This unseparated continuity of the sound is an invaluable resource, in

36

music of any period including the baroque, when any *one* note has a duration such that it cannot be sustained with comfort, or at all, in a single full bow. It is, of course, a necessary skill to be able to move the bow very slowly while still maintaining a soft but singing tone which does not sound grudging or inhibited; and in some passages this is just the effect required. But there are strict limits on how far this can be carried; and well before the limits are approached, it is usually better to make an imperceptible change of bow. This keeps plenty of control and suppleness in reserve.

When, however, consecutive but distinct notes are repeated at the same pitch, it may be a great error of judgement to connect them so smoothly that they sound like one note, thus obliterating the intended pattern. This is a fairly common fault in baroque performances today, and particularly unfortunate there, because separation between the subdivisions of the phrase is so important in making clear the meaning of a baroque melody; and because even within these subdivisions, articulation of individual notes of the *same* pitch should often be quite apparent.

Another use for this unseparated continuity of the sound is to join *different* notes with the smoothest possible legato. It is the most usual requirement of baroque slow movements that they should be taken with a true cantabile, and a true singer's continuity of line and melody: impeccably moulded; unfailingly sustained.

We shall return later to the methods by which this melodic line has to be separated into its constituent patterns by clear enough phrasing; but the patterns themselves must sing through, and for this the violin must be able to join notes in perfect legato, not only when slurred in the same bow stroke, but also when taken with consecutive strokes.

3 The violinist's détaché

Consecutive strokes of the bow, when taken legato on the violin, are called détaché, 'detached'. But this refers only to the fact that detached strokes are used, as opposed to slurs. The sound is not intended to be detached, but on the contrary, as smoothly legato as possible. And that, of course, is very smooth indeed.

The détaché stroke, i.e. legato, has undoubtedly its uses in baroque music; but there is one important reservation to be noticed. In classical music of the nineteenth century, and still more in romantic music, there is every expectation that a succession of notes, mainly similar and moderate in value, will (if they are intended to be smooth) be well suited by the ordinary modern violinist's legato; and the proper stroke for them will be the détaché. In baroque music, and perhaps also in classical music of the eighteenth century, that is not quite the expectation. For modern performers, the ordinary manner of connection, other things being equal, is expected to be legato: that is the standard situation, from which any degree of staccato is the departure. But for baroque performers, the ordinary manner of connection, other things being equal, was not legato: nor was it staccato; it was somewhere in between.

F. W. Marpurg, writing in terms of harpsichord technique, put it thus (*Anleitung*, Berlin, 1755, 2nd ed. 1765, I, vii, 29): 'Opposed to legato as well as to staccato is the ordinary movement which consists in lifting the finger from the last key (and thus interrupting the sound) shortly before touching the next note. This ordinary movement, which is always (unless counter-indicated) understood, is never indicated.' And Daniel Gottlob Türk (*Klavierschule*, Leipzig and Halle, 1789, Engl. trans., London, [1804], p. 36) likewise spoke of notes 'played in the common way; that is to say, neither *staccato* nor *legato*'.

Geminiani, a most celebrated virtuoso performer and composer for the violin, himself a pupil of Corelli, writing in terms of violin technique, recommended (*Art of Playing on the Violin*, London, 1751) an ordinary succession of fast or moderate notes 'to be play'd plain and the bow is not to be taken off the strings'. That is a description which certainly seems to include the modern détaché, although it also includes other strokes in which the sounds are not smoothly joined but are more or less distinctly separated: more or less staccato, 'separated'.

Thus the détaché is a perfectly proper stroke in baroque music; but it does not give in baroque music, as it does give in later classical music and still more in romantic music, the effect of being merely the normal, standard articulation for an average passage. It gives the effect, rather, of being a particularly smooth legato for a passage a little on the weighty side.

In baroque music, therefore, the détaché in its modern form should not be used for an average passage of relaxed allegro, which wants to dance along with a certain crisp and effortless vitality. The détaché should be reserved, in allegro, for those much less frequent though not altogether rare baroque passages which need weighting down with rather more deliberation, such as a smooth legato can well express. In adagio the détaché is (subject to clear phrasing at all proper places) a standard recourse.

4 The varying degrees of staccato

The détaché can be modified in any desired degree, without any radical change in the stroke, by two simple expedients, both of which lead to some degree of staccato.

As the first expedient, at each change of stroke the bow, instead of moving in the opposite direction so promptly and so smoothly that no separation of the sound is heard, can be *stopped* momentarily, while still remaining (as in Geminiani's instruction) on the string. This in itself will give a separation but not an emphasis to each successive note; for the bow merely rests on the string with no added pressure and the sound is in no way crushed out, but rings on a little throughout the moment of separation. This stroke gives the mildest possible degree of staccato; it can be very useful in baroque music.

As the second expedient, the bow can be not merely stopped, but *pressed* into the string while stopped. This added pressure crushes the string, dampens its vibrations, and silences the sound the more decisively the more the bow is pressed. So momentarily does this happen that the sound is never totally extinguished, since reverberation will carry it through to some extent: but it may seem to be so, and the degree of staccato depends upon how abruptly and even exaggeratedly this near-silence is enforced, and for how long a moment it is continued. Such a separated stroke gives a range of staccato to meet all situations, of which only the most extreme are unlikely to occur in baroque music.

When the pressure maintained through the moment of separation is considerable, the release of that pressure as the next stroke begins will give it considerable emphasis; or if the pressure is not released, but kept up through the stroke itself, the effect will be emphatic in the extreme. Any staccato beyond the mildest will give emphasis as well as separation, and this is perfectly appropriate in baroque music: except that there is most unlikely to be any occasion there for the most forcible extremes.

It should be added that the same degree of weight and pressure gives a harder staccato with a modern bow, and a more rounded staccato with a good baroque bow. Since this clear but rounded focus is exactly what so many average passages of baroque allegro require, the advantages for this purpose of using a baroque bow are quite conspicuous, although the right skill applied to the modern bow can also do very well. With either bow, the upper middle is very commonly the best part to use for separated strokes of short or moderate duration.

5 The sprung détaché

There is one other stroke in which the change of bow is to be taken on the string: but only just, since the pressure is allowed to lighten so much at the moment of separation that the bow very nearly springs off the string by its own elasticity and resilience, without quite doing so.

This stroke cannot be applied to notes of long duration: no natural springiness occurs. When the stroke is of moderate duration, there is just a slight feeling of springiness, lively without being emphatic; when the stroke is of short duration, this springiness almost amounts to a rebound (as in the spiccato bowings to be considered in the next chapter) but not quite, since as Geminiani put it, the bow is still not quite 'to be taken off the strings'. We may perhaps call this stroke the sprung détaché.

The upper middle of the bow is by far the best part of the bow to use, so far as circumstances allow, for the sprung détaché.

There is no stroke which is of more frequent and appropriate utility in baroque music than the sprung détaché. Unlike the modern détaché in baroque music, the sprung détaché does not sound like a special effect. It sounds average, standard and altogether normal for any ordinary baroque allegro. It ripples imperturbably along: neither light nor heavy; neither fussy nor perfunctory; but simply as the natural implications of the music would lead one to expect.

One consequence of the sprung détaché is that the notes on which it is used never start at full strength absolutely on the instant, nor do they finish absolutely at full strength. The note starts with momentary gentleness, rises to its full strength so rapidly and unemphatically that the ear is deceived, then finishes as gently as it began and with as little fuss or emphasis.

All that really happens is that the bow is given time enough to grip the string without the assistance of any added pressure, and likewise to release the string without any damping by added pressure. There is no actual staccato; but neither is there any indecisiveness. The natural resilience of the bow takes off a little even of that slight existing (not added) pressure which yields the mildest degree of staccato.

So little pressure remains during the moment of separation that the tone rings through almost undiminished by the change of bow. But not quite undiminished: the effect is not like the legato of the modern détaché. There is a distinct pulsation, but with no sense of interruption: in short, something resembling one note of a mild portato. If the bow sprang quite clear of the string, it would be a one-note spiccato. It is none of these things, but a stroke in its own right, somewhere between legato and staccato, and therefore probably nearer to that 'ordinary movement' or 'common way' which Marpurg called 'opposed to legato as well as to staccato' and Türk called 'neither staccato nor legato'.

The sprung détaché is one of the possibilities included under Geminiani's description, 'to be play'd plain and the Bow is not to be taken off the strings'. Geminiani speaks in the same place of a certain 'Swelling of the Sound', which on short notes seems to mean no more than that momentary gentleness of attack described above as resulting from the sprung détaché.

Leopold Mozart also wrote (*Violinschule*, Augsburg, 1756, V, 14) that such a stroke 'has necessarily to be started gently and with a certain moderation, and, without any lifting of the bow, taken with so smooth a join that even the most powerful stroke carries the already vibrating string over from one motion into another and different motion imperceptibly'. He did not mean that the separation itself should necessarily be imperceptible, but that the vibration should not perceptibly stop and start again; and this is just what the sprung détaché best achieves. The separation is perceived, but the sound carries through.

Tartini may likewise have intended this tactful baroque manner of easing the bow into each stroke without the hearer knowing it. 'Your first study, therefore' (he wrote in the letter already mentioned on p. 31 above) 'should be the true manner of holding, balancing and pressing the bow lightly, but steadily, upon the strings, in such a manner as that it shall seem to breathe the first tone it gives, which must proceed from the friction of the string, and not from percussion, as by a blow given with a hammer upon it. This depends on laying the bow lightly upon the string, at the first contact', after which it 'can scarce have too much force given to it, because, if the tone is begun with delicacy, there is little danger of rendering it afterwards either coarse or harsh.'

But we may turn to Leopold Mozart again to remind us (V, 3) that this is not an effect which should catch the hearer's attention. 'Every note, even the most powerfully attacked, has a small though barely audible softness at the start of the stroke; for otherwise no note would result. This same softness must also be heard at the end of every stroke.' But heard rather from the absence of any abruptness than as an effect itself; for as he says, it is 'barely audible'.

Anything conspicuous, any sort of a lunging sforzato, any bouncing or jerking or striving or fading away would merely defeat the object of the sprung détaché. The object of the sprung détaché is simply to sound normal in a baroque style: normally flowing, and normally distinct, on baroque standards.

The sprung détaché can be done well enough with the modern bow, but better with the baroque bow. For with the modern bow, it is difficult though not impossible to prevent the stick from bouncing rather too springily. One of two things may then happen: either a normal spiccato will result; or there will be a sense of constraint and rigidity caused by preventing a normal spiccato from resulting. In neither event will the typical relaxation of the sprung détaché itself be occurring. It can, indeed, be made to occur with the modern bow; but it is not altogether natural for it to occur.

It is altogether natural for the sprung détaché to occur with a good baroque bow. The edges of the sound are then beautifully rounded off: neither hard, nor soft, but just nicely focused in between.

The articulation is slightly more defined by the restrained springiness of the sprung détaché than by plain, mildly separated strokes of the same length and speed in the same part of the bow : ordinarily, the upper middle. But the difference between these strokes is no more than this slight touch of added vitality. So soon as the springiness catches any particular attention, it is too much. By comparison, even the spiccato is a special effect.

Normality is the very essence of the sprung détaché, which is useful in baroque music precisely because it does not sound there like a special effect.

CHAPTER VII

Bowings off the String

1 The difference between orchestral, chamber and virtuoso fiddling

The strokes discussed in the previous chapter are taken with the bow left on the string at the connection between one stroke and the next. The connection can be smooth and the change of bow immediate (i.e. legato, as in the modern détaché); or the connection can be more or less distinct and the change of bow momentarily delayed, during which delay there may be no added pressure (i.e. mild staccato) or there may be more or less added pressure (i.e. more or less marked staccato); or again, the springiness of the bow may be allowed to lighten the pressure of its own accord (i.e. midway between legato and staccato, as in the sprung détaché).

All these strokes can be regarded as commonplaces of baroque fiddling, equally useful in orchestral string parts, in chamber music such as trio sonatas, and in solos with any degree of virtuoso possibilities. But the strokes next to be described are taken off the string; and that always makes for something of a special effect.

Strokes taken off the string can never quite be regarded as commonplaces in baroque fiddling as a whole. They can, however, be regarded as commonplaces in baroque virtuoso fiddling. This is a distinction to which we must now give attention.

We have spoken of the most general qualities which are common to all styles of baroque fiddling, and ought never to be absent from our baroque performances: the transparent sonority; the crisp articulation.

The detailed applications of these general qualities have naturally to vary according to the situation. This is a matter both of technique and of style. The mere gap in technique between average orchestral players earning a modest living in the theatre pit for opera or as ripieni parts ('stuffing') in concerti grossi, on the one hand, and the brilliant virtuosi with international reputations as composers, performers and teachers, on the other hand, was very wide in the baroque period.

A regular baroque orchestral player might range from doubtfully competent to very good and professional indeed; but his technique was certainly expected to be less extensive than he would require in the same position today. A great baroque virtuoso had the technique at his command which could do equal justice to Bach's unaccompanied violin solos and Locatelli's audacious fireworks; and his resources included almost every trick of the bow or sleight of fingering which is now available or, indeed, is physically obtainable.

Style is inseparable from technique; and it will usually sound a little out of style to use technical resources in baroque orchestral parts, or in the simpler chamber music parts, which are perfectly proper in baroque music of a more complicated virtuosity. Showy solos take showy fiddling: orchestral solidity does not. Chamber music has two natures, one brilliant and the other profound, and they may be blended in ever-varying proportions. The appropriate technique will depend upon the prevailing style.

The strokes next to be described belong rather to the virtuoso practices than to the bread-and-butter practices of the baroque period. They are therefore mainly inadvisable in any baroque orchestral part of an average, straight-forward kind. They are only appropriate in baroque trio sonatas and other chamber music where the part has genuine elements of virtuoso display, as may sometimes but by no means always happen. They are appropriate and necessary above all in those brilliant solos into which a great violinist has introduced the best of his virtuosity, with the perfectly legitimate purpose of giving scope to his own personal arts of showmanship.

In any genuinely virtuoso passage, wherever it may occur, the following strokes are available. They are grouped together for convenience here, as all taken off the string at the moment of connection. For this reason, none of them has the smoothness of legato. They separate notes with varying degrees of emphasis and prominence.

2 The varying degrees of spiccato

Of this group of bowings taken off the string, by far the most valuable and commonly appropriate in baroque music is that known as spiccato, 'picked out'.

Like the sprung détaché, the spiccato uses the natural resilience of the bow to gain a kind of self-perpetuating springiness which is allowed to rebound from stroke to stroke at the moment of connection. But the spiccato lets this springiness carry the bow right off the string and into the air: a short distance for the milder and less conspicuous degrees of spiccato; a greater distance for the stronger and more conspicuous degrees of spiccato.

Like the sprung détaché, the spiccato cannot be applied to notes of long duration: no springiness then occurs, because the rebound cannot perpetuate itself beyond quite small limits of time and space. Unlike the sprung détaché, the spiccato in its natural form cannot be applied even to notes of moderate duration: not enough springiness then occurs to lift the bow clear of the string, but only to release a little of the pressure.

But the spiccato can be extremely well applied to notes of rather short or very short duration. Lightly done, it can join them together like pearls on a thread. Powerfully done, it can pick them out (the literal meaning of *spiccare*) with an almost but not quite percussive emphasis. Delicate in pianissimo or in piano, dazzling in forte, the spiccato is one of the most beautiful and versatile strokes a violinist has. It is not available in fortissimo, since when done with the force required for that it turns into the more energetic stroke best distinguished as jeté, 'thrown' (for which see below). In every other nuance, the spiccato is a stroke which can combine great brilliance with perfect dignity, and is very valuable indeed in suitable passages of baroque music.

The upper middle, or the actual middle, are normally the best parts of the bow in which to take the spiccato stroke.

Geminiani (in his *Art of Playing on the Violin*, already cited) probably intended the spiccato when he described 'a Staccato, where the Bow is taken off the Strings at every Note'. He considered it a valuable stroke, but only as a deliberate and not entirely usual effect, on notes of somewhat short duration. And Geminiani, of course, was a virtuoso of virtuosos.

Some modern violinists may prefer to use more spiccato than others in ordinary, not especially virtuoso passages of baroque music. This is neither unhistorical, nor necessarily inartistic. We may simply put it that the plainer the part, the less its natural compatibility with fancy bowings; and in baroque music, the spiccato is to some extent a fancy bowing. Hence the recommendation here to try the sprung détaché for the great majority of average passages, reserving the spiccato for passages in which some element of virtuosity more obviously calls for it.

3 The modern violinist's jeté

The sprung détaché uses the natural springiness of the bow without actually allowing it to rebound. The spiccato uses the natural springiness of the bow to get it to rebound. But the jeté or 'thrown' stroke does not only rely on the natural springiness of the bow. The player raises the bow further from the string into the air, and throws it back again, by the deliberate use of muscular power, thus causing a more violent rebound, and a greater degree of separation and emphasis, than would otherwise occur.

The jeté can only be used for notes of short duration, since the rebound will be as quick as it is violent. But since it is not self-perpetuating, being under deliberate muscular control, the next stroke can be delayed at will, and the *separation* between the notes thereby prolonged, to any degree which still makes good musical sense. It is possible to effect in this way the graceful equivalent of a staccato so extreme in the length of the separation that it could not possibly sound anything but harsh if the bow were held down against the string.

The jeté is not available in pianissimo, since when done with the delicacy required for that it could be no more thrown on to the string than happens involuntarily in spiccato. In piano, it is exhilarating; in forte, it is hard; in fortissimo, it is strident.

Though valuable in some classical and much romantic music, the jeté is probably quite out of character in any baroque music with the exception of decidedly bravura solos.

4 The modern violinist's martelé

The martelé or 'hammered' stroke might be described as a jeté or 'thrown' stroke without the rebound, which is deliberately suppressed. It is a more ponderous and percussive manner of attack than any other, and when held pressed into the string during the moments of separation, produces a harsher staccato. When lifted during the moment of separation, the martelé is no longer so ponderous, but it continues to be percussive.

The martelé has a somewhat bizarre effect in pianissimo and in piano; a formidable effect in forte; an overwhelming effect in fortissimo. It is altogether too strenuous a stroke for any continuous application in baroque music.

The martelé is at much its most powerful when taken at the heel of the bow; and at the present time, this stroke is often used continuously for a vigorous baroque allegro. But this is to introduce far too much sense of effort for good baroque fiddling style. The stroke for such a movement can be just as strong as may be desired; but it should preferably be a sprung détaché in the upper middle of the bow. This applies to violins, violas, cellos and basses alike.

The martelé may not have been a baroque stroke at all. David Boyden, in his magnificent *History of Violin Playing* (London, 1965), could not confirm its existence before the late eighteenth century, and thinks it did not come in before about 1750. The baroque bow is not nearly so well adapted as the modern bow for producing the martelé. Tartini condemned it almost by name when he wrote (letter quoted on p. 31 above) that the beginning of each note 'must proceed from the friction of the string, and not from percussion, as by a blow given with a hammer upon it'.

The martelé is one of the very few strokes which it may be desirable to exclude from our technique in performing baroque music. This is particularly true of the martelé taken at the heel throughout a long-continued passage: we might say of this, almost certainly, that it never happened in the baroque period; and quite certainly, that it makes an inartistic as well as anachronistic effect in the vast majority of baroque passages to which it is now customarily applied.

The strenuousness which is the deliberate purpose of the martelé is not inartistic in its proper context, as for example in Brahms, or still more in Bartók. But any such strenuousness, however produced, is contrary to those general qualities of baroque performing style which have been here described: its transparent sonority; its crisp articulation.

CHAPTER VIII

Notes under a Slur

1 Notes under a slur joined or separated

Notes under a slur are taken in one bow, except when the slur is so long that an imperceptible change of bow is necessary or at least desirable. In that case, the slur is showing its other function, as a phrase marking rather than as a bowing; but the effect to the ear should be indistinguishable.

Notes under a slur, like individually bowed notes, can either be joined smoothly, or separated more or less distinctly and emphatically. Of these strokes, by far the most importance attaches to slurring smoothly, and this is what we mean when we speak of slurred notes. But the strokes which separate the notes under the slur are also quite often useful and attractive.

Slurs of the ordinary kind which join the notes under them are part of the basic string technique of the baroque period, as of other periods. Slurs of the special kinds which separate the notes under them are part of the virtuoso string technique of the baroque period, but not, on the whole, part of the basic string technique, although there are certain such usages which do find quite an ordinary place in baroque fiddling (see p. 51f.).

2 Normal slurs

Normal slurs on bowed instruments have the same effect as normal breathing on the voice and wind instruments: unless there is a deliberate separation (by interrupting the movement of the bow without change of direction), the continuity of the sound is the greatest possible.

The number of notes within the slur may vary from two, at the least, to the largest number which a full stroke can sustain, at the most. When the next stroke is then taken without any perceptible separation, the effect to the ear may be of a slur indefinitely continued.

The frequency with which slurs were notated increased throughout the baroque period. But in baroque music, we should never wait for expression marks to appear in the notation. They do appear, and more of them appear in later than in earlier baroque music. But they were always meant to be supplied by the performer when absent, and supplemented (and modified) by him when present. Slurs are no exception to this important principle.

Even in the sixteenth century, when idiomatic techniques of composition and performance were in course of being defined for string instruments, we find Diego Ortiz in his treatise on virtuoso viol playing (*Trattado*, Rome, 1553, f.3r) advising: 'when two or three quarter-notes [crotchets] occur in one example [showing no slurs in the notation], only the first is to be defined and the others passed over without a fresh stroke of the bow'.

In the baroque period, we can unhesitatingly use slurs wherever they can gracefully be introduced, whether they are notated or not. Nevertheless, there are some reservations.

Many passages, especially in late baroque allegros, where there is a continuous succession of moderate or short notes wholly or mainly of the same value, do not imply or require slurs at all, and are not improved but merely made to sound fussy if slurs are introduced (see C. P. E. Bach, p. 50 below). Even simple, short slurs may be quite out of place; and complicated or long slurs are ruinous.

In other passages, a few short and simple slurs or even many such, may be very graceful. A pattern may be set up, for example, of two notes slurred and two notes plain (or two notes slurred and one note plain, in triple rhythm), which may be continued unaltered throughout quite a long passage. If it sounds natural, we need not be afraid of its becoming monotonous. On the contrary, it is much better to set up a good pattern and stay with it than to keep changing the pattern restlessly and pointlessly. A consistent slurring is more convincing than a complicated slurring in most ordinary passages; and short slurs (of three or four or six notes) are more convincing than long slurs.

In virtuoso passages, a complicated slurring may be genuinely in keeping with the implications of the music, and may add brilliantly to the effect of it. We very commonly find patterns such as three slurred, three plain (fairly simple), or five slurred, one plain (more tricky) or six slurred, six plain, or eight slurred, eight plain, or the like, shown in the notation, but not consistently shown. It is then for us to take the hint; and to carry the slurring through more consistently in performance than is perhaps indicated in the notation.

3 Slurs in baroque music

Expression marks in baroque music are always more in the nature of hints than of obligations. Even J. S. Bach, who could play the violin and notated many interesting as well as some bewildering slurrings, was not really at all careful in the matter, relying, as he and his contemporaries habitually did, on the performers to work out their own details of interpretation from the quite incomplete hints which might or might not be included in the notation. It is quite in order for us to modify Bach's bowings, and very necessary for us to complete them: he would have expected it of us, although we shall obviously start from his own suggestions.

On the other hand, we should never assume that a baroque passage can only be made interesting by elaborate slurrings and complicated bowings. It is the phrasing which makes a passage interesting, not the bowings: these may bring a touch of added brilliance in the right places; in the wrong places, they are nothing but a distraction; and in no place are they nearly so important as a clear and meaningful nuancing of the notes themselves.

In baroque music, it is always the line which matters most. Sustain the line in its great arches of sound, mould it and shape it and divide it into its constituent patterns: that is what brings the real dividends. Any additional elegance from complex bowings is the merest bonus.

4 Baroque advice on slurring

'It is necessary', wrote Quantz (*Essay*, Berlin, 1752, VII, 10), not to rely on indications in the notation, but 'to study how to detect and understand well what makes musical sense, and what must be joined together. It is necessary to avoid, with equal care, separating what belongs together, and joining what comprises more than one thought and should therefore be separate.' And in particular (XI, 10): 'It is necessary to avoid slurring notes which ought to be detached and detaching notes which ought to be slurred.' There may be no slurs marked at all; but if, for example, the first figure in a sequence (XVIII, ii, 5), 'is marked with a slur, they must all be played in the same way'.

And C. P. E. Bach wrote (*Essay*, Berlin, I, 1753, III, 5): 'In general, the liveliness of allegros is conveyed by detached notes, and the feeling of adagios by sustained, slurred notes . . . even when not so marked. . . . I realize, however, that every style of performance may occur at any tempo.'

Leopold Mozart wrote (*Violinschule*, Augsburg, 1756, V, 14): 'You must therefore be at pains, where the singingness of the piece requires no separation, not only to leave the bow on the violin at the change of stroke, in order to bind one stroke to another, but also to take many notes in one stroke, and in such a way that the notes which belong together shall run one into another, and be distinguished in some degree merely by loud and soft.'

5 The portato for convenience

It is frequently convenient to take two strokes consecutively in the same direction: two down bows in succession; or two up bows in succession. The convenience lies in getting to the part of the bow desired for the next notes, and in the desired direction of stroke.

This can be done in two ways. The first, which is the easiest in most contexts, is simply to stop the bow for the required moment of separation, pressing as lightly or as heavily on the string as desired for the required degree of staccato if any; and then to go on in the same direction, for the second part of the combined stroke.

This is, in effect, a portato of two notes in one stroke, so managed that it serves as two strokes in the same direction. It is a normal baroque recourse, both for down strokes and for up strokes; and it was in particular a recourse of that French style of fiddling which Georg Muffat helped to bring to Germany after his stay in Paris studying Lully's well-drilled orchestra.

The object of this French style was to take down beats (and accented notes) down bow, and up beats (and unaccented notes) up bow, with the greatest possible consistency; whereas the Italian style paid less regard to this general principle, and was more inclined to let the bowings go on as they fall out unless this brings a whole passage upside down. But that was only a difference of degree. Putting the bowing right by taking two strokes consecutively in the same direction is an extremely common and useful recourse in any baroque music.

The other way of doing this is no mere matter of convenience, and is a little more difficult: it is not merely to stop the bow during the moment of separation, but to lift it up and bring it back to the same part of the bow at which the (first) stroke began, then taking the (second) stroke over again in the same direction. This is not really two strokes combined in one; it is two strokes identically repeated in the same part of the bow, but separated by the time taken to bring the bow back again (clear of the string) to the same starting-point.

The object of these strokes identically repeated may include the convenience of getting to the part of the bow desired for the next notes, and in the desired direction of stroke. But the deliberate effect is always a special one, giving to the separation a peculiar flavour of vehemence which cannot quite be got by any other stroke. It is a magnificent effect in its own striking yet perfectly baroque fashion, and it has already been suggested (see p. 33 above) as an excellent bowing, both in convenience and in artistic result, for the main theme of the last movement of J. S. Bach's Fourth Brandenburg Concerto.

But it has, of course, nothing musically to do with the portato stroke.

6 The portato for special effect

However, the portato stroke itself can also be used not merely for convenience but for special effect, and was so used in the baroque period.

Two notes, three notes, four notes or six notes (but scarcely more), of moderate or rather short duration, can be taken in one bow (down, or up, or proceeding down and up alternately); they are articulated by stopping for just a sufficient moment of separation, with just sufficient pressure of the bow on the string, to give them a kind of throbbing pulsation.

It is this pulsation which makes the true portato a different effect from any imitation of it merely by taking successive bow strokes for each note. There is an impulse pushing on through the entire group of notes within the stroke, and giving them a connection in the very act of articulating them.

This is particularly telling when the notes of each group, and often of successive groups, are wholly or largely at the same pitch. If the note is chromatically altered within the group, then this chromatic note can be given a slightly increased stress within the overall impetus, very conducive to the expression.

Altogether the portato is an expressive resource in baroque music, and one which does not have to be confined to virtuoso passages. There are many orchestral passages (especially on throbbing chords), and some passages in trio sonatas, which invite the portato, and are the better for it. Occasionally it is notated, by slurs over groups of notes bearing staccato signs; but like most good baroque effects it is at the disposal of the performer whether there is anything in the notation to suggest it or not.

7 Spiccato reiterated within the stroke

When the bow is allowed to rebound, as in the individual spiccato, but is then continued in the same direction, we have not a portato but a spiccato reiterated within the stroke.

This multiple spiccato, even more than the individual spiccato, is a virtuoso stroke. Not every virtuoso approved of the effect; but it was already familiar when Jean Rousseau (*Traité de la Viole*, Paris, 1687, p. 73) condemned on the viol 'those runs up and down the instrument with rebounding bow which are called "Ricochets", and which are hardly bearable on the violin'. A still more celebrated viola da gamba soloist, Marin Marais (*Pièces*, II, Paris 1701), used a slur with dots as a sign 'to articulate all these notes, in one bow, as if they were played with different bowings', which might mean portato if the speed is moderate, but spiccato if the speed is faster.

Leopold Mozart (*Violinschule*, Augsburg, 1756, I, iii, 16) used dots to show 'that the notes under the slur are not only to be taken in one bow-stroke but have also to be separated from each other by a slight pressure' (i.e. portato); and dashes to show that 'the bow is lifted for each note' (i.e. either jeté or spiccato according to circumstances, spiccato being the most probable). But dots and dashes were used interchangeably, where they were used at all, in most baroque notation. These decisions as to bow stroke and playing style were almost always left to be taken not by the composer (and still less by the editor, since this species of musician had hardly yet come into being) but by the performer. We as modern editors or modern performers have to do something about it now.

The duration of notes which can be taken as spiccato reiterated within the stroke ranges from moderate to very short (perhaps the commonest are rather short); the number varies with the player's skill, but is quite considerable. Piano and forte are excellent; pianissimo is doubtful, and fortissimo is impossible.

There are probably no baroque orchestral parts which call for this quite special effect, and few if any trio sonata parts; but virtuoso solo parts may be freely allowed it. Leopold Mozart (VI, 11) gives examples of two notes to a stroke taken both down bow and up bow; but his examples of longer groups of notes, taken as spiccato reiterated within the stroke, are shown up bow only. And indeed, a good down bow multiple spiccato is a very difficult accomplishment, which some fine violinists never manage to perfect. It can also be very beautiful when it is perfected, however; and both up bow and down bow spiccato are valid baroque resources in a genuinely virtuoso context.

CHAPTER IX

Other Nuances of Bowing

1 Varieties of accent

We come now to (g), other nuances of bowing, including accentuation and dynamic shading.

Many of the strokes already discussed carry their own consequences for accentuation, but not all do so, and we have then a choice of methods.

Accents can be made with the bow by *weight*, by *pressure*, by *speed* or by *bite*; or by some combination of these.

The heaviest accents use the full weight of the arm powerfully assisted by muscular pressure. In order to bring full power to bear, they may be taken jeté or martelé; but even when taken on the string, they are more powerful than anything in baroque music is likely to require or to justify. The foregoing are extreme weight-with-pressure accents.

A strong but not excessive accent for baroque music is produced by pressure exerted on the string at the very start of the note, but released just as the bow gets into motion. The release of the pressure adds a sharp bite to the beginning of the sound; and the combination is not only very effective but very well suited to many baroque idioms. These are pressure-with-bite accents.

A more gentle and suave accent can be produced by making the pressure less strong and the release of it less sudden. This will often do very well in baroque slow movements. These are bite accents.

When speed is added to the combination, an element of restlessness enters in, especially if the increased speed and pressure of the bow occur at the start of the note, returning to normal shortly afterwards. This is primarily a speed-with-pressure accent; and it is not very likely to be a suitable baroque accent. But if the increased speed and pressure of the bow occur not at the start, but just afterwards, then we have the true sforzando: a speed-with-pressure accent, not before but while the stroke gains momentum.

2 The sforzando

The true sforzando is a perfectly suitable form of accentuation in many baroque situations, and indeed it was fashionable to the point of abuse in some schools. Caccini (*Nuove Musiche*, Florence, 1602, Introd.) prescribed it for singers, with reservations; while Geminiani (*Art of Playing on the Violin*, London, 1751) apparently advocated it for violinists rather indiscriminately, though his description is far from clear and he may have meant nothing more than the almost imperceptible impulse which marks the start of the sprung détaché.

It is not only in baroque music that the sforzando, although valuable, is liable to abuse. It is a strong recourse, and an easy one to fall back upon as an artifice when genuine expression is lacking. When felt from the heart, it is a wonderful means of intensifying the peak note of a phrase, particularly if this note is delayed minutely by a tiny silence of articulation, and then placed very purposefully and deliberately at the climax. When it becomes an unnoticed mannerism on every long or moderate note, the sforzando forms a habit as hard to cure as some singers' 'intrusive aitch', and quite as irritating. The sforzando needs to be under firm control; but when it is, its value in baroque music at the right places can be very high.

3 The bite accent

The most valuable of all accents for baroque music, however, depends very little on weight, pressure or speed of the bow, and almost entirely on bite. A very slight pressure is put on to the stick by the forefinger. This causes the hair to bite keenly but not heavily; and it is the release of this bite which gives the accent, as the pressure is lightened in the very act of starting the movement of the bow.

The bite accent can be strengthened by increasing the initial pressure, and lightened by decreasing the initial pressure. It is crisp, not massive; and when an entire passage of moderate or rather short notes wants sharpening up a little, a touch of this crispness can be given to every note. The merest momentary pressure of the forefinger on the stick added just at the start, and immediately released, will do it; and this technique is particularly effective when combined with the sprung détaché. The stroke then remains no less easy and relaxed, but it is given a sharp cutting edge, very much in the baroque character.

4 The agogic accent

The effect sometimes called an agogic accent is also in the baroque character, and is as valuable in baroque music as it is elsewhere. It is not strictly an accent at all, although it can be combined with an accent; for in itself it is not a dynamic intensification, but a slight prolongation of the peak note of a phrase for expressive emphasis. Its effect can be further increased by slightly delaying the note itself, through a momentary silence of articulation in front of it, so that it is placed not quite punctually but all the more tellingly for having been thus momentarily held back.

Like the sforzando, the agogic accent must be used sparingly and from the heart; but it is an important feature of good phrasing, and very necessary for this purpose in baroque music.

5 Baroque accents seldom coincide merely with the beat

In baroque music, there is more likelihood than in renaissance music that the accentuation will basically follow the metre, and in all parts alike. Metrical accentuation of this kind requires, as a rule, very little dynamic or agogic stressing, but merely such as any good musician will give it naturally. Metrical accentuation looks after itself; but even in baroque music, it does not consistently coincide with that expressive accentuation which must come deliberately from the musician, and which may sometimes reinforce but sometimes override the metrical expectation.

This is what Geminiani had in mind when he warned us (*Art of Playing on the Violin*, London, 1751, p. 9): 'If by your manner of bowing you lay a particular Stress on the Note at the Beginning of every Bar, so as to render it predominant over the rest, you alter and spoil the true Air [as we might say, phrasing] of the Piece.' And it was Schweitzer who in modern times so perceptively urged us (*Jean Sébastian Bach*, Paris, 1905, Ger. ed. Leipzig, 1908, Eng. trans. E. Newman, London, 1911, II, 381) to look for the peak note of a phrase (generally its highest note) on whatever beat, and to give that note the expressive accent; for this, as Leopold Mozart suggested (*Violinschule*, Augsburg, 1756, XII, 13) 'is generally taken on the highest notes'. We must decide to which note the phrase is going, and shape our phrasing to go to that note too. It is not enough for the player to know, as most good players do know; it is also necessary that he should make his separations and his accents, his lingerings and his postponements sufficiently big for the listeners to grasp the patterns. In actual performance, there is a frequent tendency to underphrase the patterns in baroque music, though it is also possible, of course, to make too much of them.

6 Dynamic nuances within the stroke

Bowings can be nuanced dynamically within the stroke as well as at the beginning of it. There are such innumerable shadings too slight for any deliberate calculation or written notation, but learnt from good example and good intuition. These are just as important in baroque music as in any other. A dead-pan straightness of the tone is lethal to string playing, and contrary to the teaching and practice of the great baroque violinist-composers themselves.

7 The messa di voce

There is, however, one particular dynamic nuance within the stroke which was described by many baroque authorities. This is to start the bow soft, swell it to loud in the middle, and shade it off to soft again by the end. It was an effect borrowed from the bel canto singers, who cultivated it to prodigious extremes of contrast and control; their name for it was *messa di voce*, literally, 'placing of the voice'.

The *messa di voce* became exaggerated by the singers, with whom this genuinely expressive effect reached a point of affectation which we need feel no wish to emulate. In the later baroque period, the virtuoso violinists imitated not only the effect but also the affectation; yet when judiciously applied it is a wonderful stroke on long notes which, falling in a context of shorter notes, might otherwise seem a little bald and unconvincing.

An excellent example of a passage improved by the *messa di voce* is the opening of J. S. Bach's (disputed, but unconvincingly disputed) trio sonata in C major. The whole note (semibreve) G with which the first violin opens can begin piano: not, however, pianissimo, which would not, perhaps, catch the attention of the audience sufficiently. The note can then be swelled to forte by about half-way through: not, however, to fortissimo, which would too much disturb the serenity of this essentially tranquil movement. Thereafter, the volume can be allowed to sink about to mezzo-forte, for the shorter notes which take over just after the beginning of the second bar: this being about the right dynamic level for the passage as a whole.

Meanwhile, the continuo accompaniment part and the bass part in striding eighth notes (quavers) on which this accompaniment is to be realized, should both of them *begin* mezzo-forte, and maintain that level all through the first violin's *messa di voce*: they must not let themselves get drawn into the dynamic nuance in the melodic part.

But when the second violin enters two bars later with the same theme a fifth lower, beginning on a whole note C similarly tied over just into the following bar, the same nuance should be repeated: the entry piano; the swell to forte in the middle; the decline to mezzo-forte by the end. But now neither the first violin nor the continuo must get drawn into the second violin's nuance. They must remain imperturbably mezzo-forte throughout. It is now the second violin which will first enter almost unnoticed at a lower dynamic level than theirs, next stand out above them at a higher dynamic level, then drop to the same dynamic level for the continuation of the passage.

It should be mentioned that no dynamic marking of any kind is notated in the original manuscript of this entire sonata. The entire expressive scheme is left in typical baroque fashion to the performer. We have merely to follow the implications of the music; but of course, it is very important that we should do so responsively.

8 Pizzicato

In pizzicato, bowing is temporarily suspended in favour of direct plucking of the string by one or other finger, or the thumb, of the right hand; or occasionally, for a short pizzicato note or two interspersed too rapidly among bowed notes for the right hand to get there in time, by a momentarily disengaged finger of the left hand.

Pizzicato effects of all varieties (including the left-hand pizzicato) were familiar throughout the baroque period, and the techniques seem to have been no different from our own. But they were mainly resources of the soloists (including unaccompanied solos on the bass viol tuned lyra-wise to facilitate a great variety of chords).

Orchestral pizzicato was nevertheless employed, at least occasionally, and perhaps more often than we suppose. Monteverdi asked for it specifically in his famous *Combattimento* of 1624, with the instruction: 'here one leaves the bow and one plucks the strings' and 'here one takes up the bow again'. There are other such indications found through the baroque period; and, of course, in such a matter we do not have to wait to be told, but can do it for ourselves at our own discretion.

A Vivaldi slow movement, for example, with its purposeful bass part taken pizzicato throughout, is quite telling and quite acceptable. Yet we may possibly conclude that it may be yet more telling and acceptable with the bass part bowed as usual, and with all the usual melodic nuancing which bowing permits. Pizzicato passages in all the strings are also telling and acceptable as a special effect. It is simply that judgement is required, and that, on the whole, pizzicato is likely to be a great deal rarer in baroque performances than in later contexts (where, if wanted, it is almost certain to be notated).

9 Muting the strings

The same judgement and the same reticence is recommended in the use of the mute. As a matter of history, no objections can arise: it was used, and sometimes even indicated, in the baroque period. As a matter of artistry, very few baroque movements or passages are really improved by this rather gimmicky effect: a good transparent pianissimo unmuted is quite a different sound, of course, and may not always be the right sound; but in nearly every case, it probably is.

10 Bowing for three-part and four-part chords

The majority of three-part and four-part chords in baroque violin music have no need to be struck or held down simultaneously. In so far as this can be done with no sense of strain, it is not ruled out; but this is difficult for three-part chords, and impossible for four-part chords.

A curvature of the bridge so low as to make simultaneous three-part chords easy, and four-part chords possible, would be too low to allow single strings to be played forte without unavoidably touching the neighbouring strings when only one note is needed.

A bow with its hair so relaxed as to curl around three or four strings at once, thus sounding full harmony like a hurdy-gurdy, never existed in the baroque period or any other period until our own when an unfortunate scholarly misconception by Arnold Schering (which he soon withdrew but which had meanwhile been taken up in error by the influential Albert Schweitzer) led to the purely modern invention of hoop-shaped bows designed to do this when a trigger is released by the bow-hand thumb, and to be normally stiff when the trigger is turned the other way.

But nothing, unfortunately, is farther from Bach than these so-called 'Bach bows', the effect of which is very interesting, very strange, and one hundred per cent removed from anything which did happen, could have happened or ought to happen in any baroque music whatsoever.

The ordinary baroque method of performing chords and polyphony on the violin was as Jean-Philippe Rameau (*Pièces de clavecin en concerts*, Paris, 1741, preface) explained it: 'at places where one cannot easily perform two or more notes together, either one arpeggiates them, stopping on that [note] from the side of which the melody continues; or one gives the preference, sometimes to the notes at the top, sometimes those at the bottom'.

Jean-Jacques Rousseau was in disagreement with Rameau on almost every subject, but in full agreement on this; for Rameau supported the French style, and Rousseau the Italian style. Thus both these leading baroque styles were evidently alike in their ordinary method of performing chords on the violin. Rousseau (*Dictionnaire*, Paris, 1768, 'Arpeggio') explained the 'manner of performing the different notes in rapid succession instead of striking them at once. There are instruments on which a chord cannot be produced except by arpeggiation; instruments such as the violin, the cello and the viol, and all those played with a bow, because the convexity of the bridge prevents the bow from pressing on all the strings at once.'

This would seem to be in general the best solution. Just as polyphony on the lute is often rather sketchy in the notes played, but sounds complete because the mind supplies the implied polyphonic continuity, so the suites for unaccompanied violin by Walther or Biber or J. S. Bach himself do not need to have (and sometimes cannot have) every note physically sounding which is notated in the polyphony. It is much more important to keep the texture limpid and the sound relaxed; the mind will supply anything in the part-writing which is physically missing in the performance. This is big music, none bigger; but at the least sign of being forced, it merely sounds uncomfortable. The serenest performance will serve its bigness best.

CHAPTER X

Left-hand Colouring

1 Left-hand technique in baroque music

The technique of the left hand, as mentioned on p. 27, influences the *sonority* of the violin:

    (h) by choice of fingerings (see below);

    (i) choice of position (see p. 62);

    (j) by strength of impact (see p. 65);

    (k) by degree of portamento if any (see p. 65);

    (l) by degree of vibrato if any (see p. 66).

The factor of impact and the factor of portamento also influence the *articulation*.

    The primary function of the left hand is to stop the strings and make the notes. So difficult is this function to perfect that the importance is sometimes underestimated of the secondary function of the left hand, in colouring the sound and moulding it to match and enhance the beauties imparted by the right hand with its techniques of bowing. But fingering, shifting and above all vibrato make contributions which are much more than utilitarian; and we shall want these contributions to be as well in keeping with baroque style as the contributions of the bowing hand.

2 Fingerings

(h) Choice of fingerings often arises between taking a note stopped and taking it on an open string.

    Modern practice tends to avoid open strings except when the convenience of a momentary open string outweighs the slight change of colouring. This was also, up to a point, the practice of the virtuoso baroque violinists. Leopold Mozart (*Violinschule*, Augsburg, 1756, VIII, i, 13) wrote that 'a soloist will do well to allow his open strings to sound rarely or not at all. His fourth finger on the next lower string will always sound more unobtrusive and refined, since the open strings are too loud compared with stopped notes, and penetrate the ear too keenly.'

But for orchestral parts and most trio sonata parts this rule does not in the least apply. On the contrary, the momentary robustness of the open string conforms very well with the clear colourings which are of the essence of average baroque string playing. The more veiled and poetical colourings are in keeping rather with the advanced solo styles of the later baroque violinist-composers than with the orchestral and chamber styles, or even with the solo styles of the early and the middle portions of the baroque period.

3 Positions

(i) This difference between virtuoso and ordinary performance is still more important with regard to choice of position. Leopold Mozart added (V, 13): 'In the same way, a soloist should make a point of taking all feasible passages on one string, in order to keep them in one tone-colouring.' In Vivaldi, Tartini or Geminiani, positions up to the seventh were standard; and they were taught, without any special comment, in Geminiani's *Art of Playing on the Violin* (London, 1751).

Higher positions up to the tenth (L'Abbé le fils, i.e. J. B. Saint-Sevin, *Principes du violon*, Paris, [1761]) were regarded as exceptional, but available; up to the fourteenth (Locatelli, Op. 3, *L'Arte del violino*, Amsterdam, [1733]) as indubitably a little freakish. The highest of these positions (from around the seventh position) are right off the end of the average eighteenth century fingerboard, but can be stopped without fingerboard. Their effect, of course, is very far from standard.

'Consistency of tone colouring is achieved', said Leopold Mozart (VIII, i, 2), through using higher positions on lower strings rather than crossing to a higher string, 'as well as a more even and singing execution.' This is perfectly true, and is exactly what the more showy solos of the late baroque fiddlers require. But when Leopold Mozart was thinking of average orchestral and chamber performances, he spoke (II, 5) of that 'honest and manly' tone, or (V, 12) of that 'good, steady, singing and as it were round, fat tone', to which we have already given our attention (see p. 29f.).

Baroque string music which is at the same time of great virtuosity and great depth of feeling, for example the unaccompanied violin suites and cello suites of J. S. Bach, should be fingered with more regard to the lie of the phrasing than to the sensuous tone of high positions for their own sake. There should be no climbing to high positions on low strings unless the notes so taken belong in the same phrase; and this is not usually the case. Nearly always there are more real contrapuntal parts implied than are visibly notated; they can be suggested by fingering them so that the lower part lies on a lower string, the higher part on a higher string. What is in appearance one long phrase will nearly always break down like this into answering sub-phrases, each on its own string, and therefore each in a fairly low position on that string. A sense of pattern is the proper guide to this.

Average baroque orchestral parts do not require, and trio sonata parts hardly require, positions above the third position, with occasional fourth finger extension (or else momentarily fourth position) to take in (on the violin) the E an octave above the top open string. It is in this lower range of positions (which, incidentally, even the solo violin sonatas of Corelli do not exceed) that the tone of the violin can be made 'honest and manly': clear, forthright and transparent.

The inevitably veiled tone and the poetic suggestiveness of the positions above the third on the lower three strings of the violin are admirable effects (both historically authenticated and artistically appropriate) in any suitable passage of baroque music which has a virtuoso quality. The virtuoso quality was mainly though not wholly in the Italianate style, and is invariably for solo display. Where it is found to some extent in trio sonatas (for example, some of Handel's) it may be performed accordingly; but it is not basically a chamber-music style, nor is it at all an orchestral style (except for the solo parts of concerti grossi), in baroque music.

Therefore, orchestral parts, and most chamber parts, and quite often solo parts should be taken in the lower positions (i.e. up to the third position with fourth-finger extension) as a general although not invariable rule. All the bread-and-butter work of baroque fiddling was done within the limits of the third position, with free use of open strings whenever in the least convenient and sometimes by preference. That is the way it used to sound, and that is the way it sounds best today. Leopold Mozart's 'honest and manly' tone is absolutely right for the majority of average baroque contexts.

4 Manner of shifting

A special technique was required for shifting down without losing control of the violin when this was held propped loosely against the chest or the collar-bone: the thumb moves back first and the rest of the hand wriggles down after it, which does the trick, with sufficient practice and experience. But for music with much shifting, this is an inherently inferior way of holding the violin; and since the grip under the chin is just as historical and far more convenient, only the most determined experimentalists will for a moment consider doing otherwise. The modern grip, chin-rest and all, has no appreciable disadvantages for baroque fiddling, and for ordinary purposes is to be unreservedly recommended.

With the normal modern way of holding the violin (which apart from the chin-rest was also one of the baroque ways), the technique for shifting requires no alteration from our usual, except that we can use the half-position even more freely, and the second position much more freely than most modern players do.

Where a modern fiddler might be inclined to go straight from first position to third position, or from third to first, a baroque fiddler might have moved only to the second position, or through second position up to third or down to first. To judge from contemporary fingerings such as those taught by Geminiani in his *Art of Playing on the Violin* (London, 1751), baroque fiddlers did not like to make distant shifts of position in one leap, if they could cover the distance more gradually by creeping through the intermediate positions; nor did they like to go to a higher position when the next lower position would serve as well.

It is a little harder technically to find second position from first or third than it is to find third from first or first from third, but it can of course be got perfectly secure with practice, and it really is a very handy position in numerous baroque passages. It is especially useful for sequential phrases, of which the first may lie best in first position, the next in second position, and the next again in third position (or in third, second, first).

The half position is extremely useful also, but this is not nearly so neglected in modern technique as second position sometimes is. Little change in our habits should be needed here.

Finger changing on the same note was taught by Geminiani. Shifting with the same finger (especially the fourth) is a more modern convenience, but perfectly applicable in baroque music. Thumb positions were used by late baroque cellists and gambists in the same way as by modern cellists; and also on occasion by virtuoso baroque violinists, as we do not now do or need to do.

5 Harmonics

The production both of natural and of artificial harmonics was familiar to skilled baroque violinists, and there are a few virtuoso solos which exploit this quite tricky and slightly dubious effect with unabashed vulgarity. There is nothing wrong with this at the right place and time; but it is entirely foreign to the ordinary baroque ideals of sonority and dignity alike.

Leopold Mozart, brilliant virtuoso violinist though he was himself, expressed (V, 13) his unqualified disapproval of 'the so-called flageolet tones', i.e. harmonics, which he described as 'a quite ridiculous kind of music and one which fights nature herself with its incongruity of tone-colouring'. Except, therefore, in the very rare baroque passages in which harmonics are an integral feature of an effect deliberately intended by the composer, we should avoid them, whether natural or artificial, in baroque music.

Thus we may want to avoid even the easy method of obtaining the *e'''* which is the octave of the open *e''*, by extending the fourth finger and touching the mid-point of the string lightly in order to produce the natural second harmonic (or first partial) of the string. Admittedly this does no harm provided that it remains inconspicuous (as on a short note momentarily touched). But it is hardly more difficult to stop the *e'''* accurately as an ordinary note, likewise by fourth-finger extension; and the result in baroque music (perhaps in any music, except for a special effect) is just a little more stylish, and is therefore probably the better choice.

6 Impact

(j) The strength of the impact with which the fingers stop the string has a small but perceptible effect on the sound, since a powerful impact lends a slightly percussive quality to the start of the note, while a gentle impact avoids this quality. Thus it is not the sonority but the articulation which is slightly altered.

There is no difference of principle here between baroque and any other string music. Some players have habitually a more percussive impact of the fingers than other players, but it is really better to proportion the strength of the impact to the character of the music. A brilliant allegro gains from a more powerful fingering. An expressive adagio gains from a more insinuating fingering. The difference is, moreover, conducive to a mood appropriate to the situation.

The difference existed in baroque fingering; for Mersenne (*Harmonie Universelle*, Paris, 1636–7, II, iv, 183) made the broad recommendation to keep the fingers close to the fingerboard and to press hard in the interests of a good resonance. That is satisfactory advice, but the strength of the impact can still be varied, and should be varied, to suit the music. Most good modern string players will be in the habit of doing this from ordinary musicianship, whether deliberately or without particularly noticing.

7 Portamento

(k) Portamento is a word for that more or less perceptibly gliding tone which is heard in shifting from one position to another, when the shifting finger is allowed to slide towards its new place on the string rather than moving there in a clean and inaudible leap. The effect is on mood in general and on articulation in particular.

Fashions in such portamento have varied with the general change of idioms in recent years. What was a perfectly normal, acceptable and admired degree of portamento forty years ago would seem today in very bad taste; yet it was bound up with an idiom of interpretation which all hung together and was very fine, as may be heard, for example, in the wonderful recordings of Beethoven by the Lener String Quartet.

No mention of this particular branch of portamento seems to have been made in the contemporary treatises and tutors of the baroque period. As already suggested, several small shifts were on the whole preferred to one big shift; and this reduced the opportunity (and the temptation) for much audible shifting. It may have occurred not uncommonly, but in very slight degree, so that it attracted no attention. Our own shifting of position in baroque music should be mostly without portamento; but a touch of it occasionally for particular expression is so natural to the violin that it may very properly be allowed.

8 Vibrato

(1) There is no doubt whatsoever that vibrato was a normal resource for string instruments throughout the baroque period. Martin Agricola (*Musica Instrumentalis Deudsch*, Wittenberg, 1529, ed. of 1545, pp. 42–3, and Ganassi (*Regola Rubertina*, Venice, 1542, Ch. II) already taught it as a 'trembling' of the fingers. Mersenne (*Harmonie Universelle*, Paris, 1636–7, Book II, chapter on ornaments) states specifically that 'the tone of the violin' is rendered attractive 'by certain tremblings' and he subsequently states that 'the left hand must swing with great violence', though (thinking better of it) he wants this extreme vibrato 'used in moderation'.

Christopher Simpson (*Division-Violist*, London, 1659, I, 16) described an especially conspicuous variety of vibrato (used on the viol and the lute) which not only makes the stopping finger oscillate, but also the next finger 'as close and near the sounding Note as possible', so as to touch it intermittently. He classed this as a 'Grace', i.e. as an ornament, and wanted it used 'where no other Grace is concerned'. Thomas Mace (*Musick's Monument*, London, 1676, p. 109) also classed vibrato as an ornament, which he called the 'Sting'. Jean Rousseau (*Traité de la Viole*, Paris, 1687, pp. 100–1) wrote 'two fingers being pressed one against the other, the one is held on the string, and the next strikes it very lightly' (this he calls *Batement*), and also 'one finger on the fret' (that he calls *Languer*); but he further taught that some degree of vibrato

66

should be used 'in all contexts where the length of the note permits, and should last as long as the note'.

Of the virtuoso violinists, Geminiani (*Art of Playing on the Violin*, London, 1751, p. 8) wrote: 'you must press the Finger strongly upon the String of the Instrument, and move the Wrist in and out slowly and equally'; and he taught that vibrato should be 'made use of as often as possible'. Leopold Mozart (*Violinschule*, Augsburg, 1756, XI, i ff.) wrote: 'the finger is pressed strongly on the string, and one makes a small movement with the whole hand'; but he thought it 'a mistake to give every note' a vibrato, while recognizing the actual presence of 'performers who tremble on every note without exception as if they had the palsy'. He may not have liked them; but they were evidently there.

These are historical facts. Some taught, like Mersenne, an extreme vibrato done 'with great violence', but then wanted it 'used in moderation'. Some taught, like Simpson, a still more extreme two-finger vibrato, but wanted it treated actually as a grace or ornament 'where no other Grace is concerned'. Others, like Mace, called the normal one-finger vibrato a grace or ornament, which implies not using it all the time. Others again, like Rousseau and Geminiani, wanted as much vibrato as possible; while Leopold Mozart rather more moderately thought that it should not be put on 'every note'.

The artistic facts support and account for these historical facts. A very wide or slow or otherwise conspicuous vibrato is too disruptive of the natural clarity of baroque music to be used as a regular resource of expression, but has its value as a special resource: i.e. treated as an ornament like any other, and used only on notes significant enough to carry such an ornament.

A very rapid and intense vibrato is too agitating to the natural poise and balance of baroque music, and too obscuring to its natural transparency: indeed, a vibrato which is both wide and rapid has a more damaging effect than anything else in making the sound thick, opaque and altogether unsuitable for baroque fiddling. If it is combined with heavy, flat-haired, massive bowing, it takes us right back to the bad old days of weighty Bach and stodgy Handel. It will not do even as an intermittent ornament; and as a persistent colouring it would be as inartistic as it is unhistorical.

But a vibrato moderately wide and steady does not muddy the sound or agitate the mind, and is in no way incongruous with the baroque transparency or the baroque poise. On the contrary, a moderate vibrato is very necessary on string instruments, as it is with the voice, to give just that sparkle of natural vitality which is so characteristic of baroque music. The flat and uncoloured sound of string tone without any vibrato could only be long maintained in baroque music, if at all, for some quite special and rather theatrical effect, like the 'white', uncoloured voice in singing. A note or two here and there without vibrato makes a valuable contrast; but vibrato-less string tone never was and never should be a standard recourse in performing baroque music. Using no vibrato is a purely modern mistake.

On the one hand, a conspicuous vibrato serving as an expressive ornament on selected notes; on the other hand, an inconspicuous vibrato serving as natural colouring on most long or moderate notes but not necessarily short notes: this is what the baroque authorities seem sometimes to have pre-scribed, and sometimes taken for granted. They may not all have thought quite alike; but in the main, when they advised only an occasional or ornamen-tal use of vibrato, they seem to have been thinking of the conspicuous use (both of the two-finger and of the one-finger varieties), while taking the more or less continuous but inconspicuous use for granted. And when they advised the more or less continuous use of vibrato, they certainly were not thinking of the conspicuous and ornamental use (which would be artistically intoler-able if thus continued), but of the inconspicuous yet colourful use which comes naturally to the voice and the strings.

It is not very important whether we choose to use a conspicuous vibrato as an occasional ornament in baroque music, although we know that this was done, and even marked with special signs by a few French composers (for example, Marin Marais, in his *Pièces de Viole*, Paris, 1686 – , gives signs and names both to the two-finger vibrato, as *Pincé* or *Flattement*, and to the one-finger vibrato, as *Plainte*). But it is very important that we should understand the need to use a moderate vibrato as a normal though not an entirely con-tinuous left-hand colouring of the tone in baroque music.

PART THREE
The Expression

CHAPTER XI

Baroque Expression in General

1 Musicianship and musicology in baroque expression

Expression in music is fundamentally one thing, and one thing alone: responding to the implications of the music itself. Good musicianship is indispensable for this; and good musicianship is a quality which is essentially the same in our modern period as it was in the baroque period, and perhaps in any other. For we are talking here about those responses, both physical and mental, which underlie the art of music.

But the forms assumed by this underlying quality of good musicianship are not the same at different periods. Thus while we can be led by our own good musicianship, and in no other way, to whatever is most fundamental in baroque expression, we cannot be led by our own good musicianship alone to every application, and still less to every detail, of baroque expression. We need in addition sufficient historical information and scholarly reconstruction, some of the main lines of which for baroque string playing are touched upon below.

2 Baroque expression not passionless

One piece of historical information which may still come as a surprise to some modern musicians is that the baroque musicians, so far from recommending any undue reticence in the performance of their music, described their experience of music in terms of the strongest feeling. Yet they did so repeatedly; and we have to take this attitude of theirs most seriously into account.

The rich and massive impact of a Wagnerian string section will weigh too heavily on Bach or Handel, Purcell or Monteverdi. This we now know; yet these great baroque composers cannot move us as they moved their own contemporaries unless they touch our feelings just as warmly, in a different language of the emotions and a different texture of sonority and articulation. Thus any modern interpretation in which the feelings are held back and the volume is kept down is historically unauthentic and artistically insufficient. We need to be able to let go with baroque abandon in our baroque fiddling.

'Transported as it were by some Musical Fury', wrote the learned English professional Charles Butler in his *Principles of Musik* (London, 1636, p. 92) 'so that himself scarce knoweth what he doth, nor can presently give a reason for his doing'. Samuel Pepys, as an amateur enthusiast, wrote in his *Diary* (27 Feb., 1667-8) of being so 'ravished' by the music 'that neither then, nor all the evening going home, and at home, I was able to think of any thing, but remained all night transported'. Thomas Mace, a professional conservative if ever there was one, described at great length in his *Musick's Monument* (London, 1676, p. 19) how he was 'drawn into Divine Raptures' by music's 'uncontroulable Persuasions'.

These three not so staid Englishmen of the seventeenth century yielded nothing, it seems, to the Italian Angelo Berardi, who wrote in his *Ragionamenti Musicali* (Bologna, 1681, p. 87) that 'music is the ruler of the passions of the soul'; or to the Frenchman François Raguenet, who in his famous *Paralele des italiens et des françois* of 1702, translated approvingly into English, probably by J. E. Galliard (London, 1709, ed. O. Strunk, *Musical Quarterly*, XXXII, 3, p. 422) called music 'transport, enchantment and extasy of pleasure'.

The Frenchman François Couperin, so much deeper in his music than its surface elegance proclaims, in his *L'Art de toucher le clavecin* (Paris, 1716, ed. of 1717, preface) confessed himself 'more pleased with what moves me than with what astonishes me'. The Italian Geminiani, never afraid to proclaim himself the virtuoso, nevertheless in his technical *Treatise of Good Taste* (London, 1749, p. 4) advised 'the Performer, who is ambitious to inspire his audience, to be first inspired himself', so that 'his Imagination is warm and glowing'.

The Germans took up the same story with Joachim Quantz (J. S. Bach's junior only by twelve years), who in his *Essay* (Berlin, 1752, XVIII, 28) insisted upon 'a feeling soul, and one capable of being moved'; and with C. P. E. Bach, the most talented and successful of J. S. Bach's sons, who attributed his own musical insight to his father's training, and who wrote in his *Essay* (Berlin, 1753, III, 13) that 'a musician cannot move others unless he too is moved'.

And what are we to say of the commemoration concert of Handel's music, shortly after the death of that eminently successful late baroque composer: the concert of which John Mainwaring reported in his *Memoirs of Handel* (London, 1760, p. 52) that 'the audience was so enchanted with this perform- ance, that a stranger who should have seen the manner in which they were affected, would have imagined they had all been distracted'? It cannot have been a very restrained performance of Handel which had the audience so excited; and clearly if we aim too much at dignity and restraint in playing, for example, a Handel violin sonata, we shall miss out on the excitement, and sound neither authentic nor enjoyable.

3 Baroque expression not always nor everywhere the same

Nevertheless, there are many shades of musical excitement. There was the adventurous and revolutionary early baroque generation of Monteverdi, Schütz, Frescobaldi and John Bull, exploring key-relationships recklessly and giving the soloist a novel prominence; and for this, a touch of wildness in our fiddling does not come amiss. There was the middle baroque generation of sober consolidation, with Corelli or Alessandro Scarlatti restricting key-relationships more classically even while Purcell or Buxtehude retained something of the older unpredictability; here our fiddling needs to be sometimes more poised, and sometimes more wayward. There was the late baroque generation of ripe harvest, with Bach's maturity and Handel's impetus, with Couperin's lucidity and Rameau's craftsmanship, with Telemann's elegance and Vivaldi's radiance, so that we need diverse fiddling to correspond.

4 Italian impetuosity and French sweetness

Through it all ran a difference of national temperaments. Mersenne already noticed it in his *Harmonie Universelle* (Paris, 1636–7, II, vi, 356): 'The Italians', he wrote in evident admiration, 'represent as much as they can the passions and the feelings of the soul and the spirit', whereas 'our Frenchmen are content to caress the ear, and use nothing but a perpetual sweetness'.

Georg Muffat brought to Germany what he learnt both under Lully in Paris and under Corelli in Rome; but in his *Florilegium I* (Augsburg, 1695, preface) he preferred the French for their 'natural melody, with an easy and smooth tune, altogether free from superfluous artifices, extravagant ornamentations, and too frequent and harsh leaps'.

Raguenet, in that controversial *Comparison between the French and Italian Musick* (to give the title its English translation, and there was a German translation too) mentioned in Section 1 above, agreed that the French 'aim at the soft, the easy, the flowing and coherent', whereas 'the Italians venture at everything that is harsh and out of the way, but they do it like people that have a right to venture and are sure of success'; for 'as the Italians are naturally more brisk than the French, so are they more sensible of the passions and consequently express them more lively', in a manner 'so brisk and piercing, so impetuous and affecting, that the imagination, the senses, the soul and the body itself are all betrayed into a general transport'. The French 'touch the violin much finer and with a greater nicety than they do in Italy', while the Italian violinist 'is seized with an unavoidable agony; he tortures the violin; he racks his body; he is no longer master of himself, but is agitated like one possessed with an irresistible motion'.

And it was Raguenet's English translator who in 1709 added in a footnote: 'I never met with any man that suffered his passions to hurry him away so much whilst he was playing on the violin as the famous Arcangelo Corelli, whose eyes will sometimes turn as red as fire; his countenance will be distorted, his eyeballs roll as in an agony, and he gives in so much to what he is doing that he doth not look like the same man'.

The Frenchman Le Cerf de la Viéville, in the many-authored *Histoire de la Musique* (Paris, 1725, II, p. 61 and IV, p. 149) gave the same information from an opposite point of view when he asserted that 'our violins are more serene', whereas the Italian violinists 'have no other merit than that of drawing plenty of sound from their instruments'.

But the more internationally-minded German writer, Joachim Quantz (*Essay*, Berlin, 1752, X, 19) took the balanced view that since the Italians are 'less restrained' and the French 'almost too much so', we should learn 'to blend the dignity and the lucidity of the French with the light and shade of the Italian instrumentalists'. For (XVIII, 53) these are the leading nations in music, and 'other nations are ruled in their taste by these two'.

That is good advice. But we must be prepared also to differentiate, where necessary, between the impetuosity and breadth often characteristic of Italian fiddling on the one hand, and the piquancy and tenderness often characteristic of French fiddling on the other hand, in music of the baroque period.

5 Theatre, chamber and church

In the baroque literature, we read frequently of another distinction to which much contemporary importance was attached. P. F. Tosi (*Opinioni*, Bologna, 1723, trans. J. E. Galliard, London, 1742, p. 92) expressed it characteristically when 'for the Theatre' he admired a style of performance 'lively and various; for the Chamber, delicate and finish'd; and for the Church, moving and grave'. Quantz (*Essay*, Berlin, 1752, XVII, vii, 53) considered that for Church music, 'the expression as well as the tempo should be more moderate than in opera'.

The more elegant and less serious kinds of late baroque chamber music were called *galant* ('courtly' would be a good free translation); but we must not be deceived by surface elegance, when deeper purposes show through. François Couperin and J. S. Bach are two composers in whose music a galant idiom may be directed to the deepest feelings, and it is these feelings which our fiddling has to carry with a light touch, but a warm heart.

It is indeed typical of baroque music as a whole that (like Mozart a little later) it may be serious without being heavy. So, then, should be our baroque fiddling, in many varieties of idiom.

CHAPTER XII

Tempo in Baroque Music

1 A good head for tempo

Of all the elements of musical expression, none is more crucial than tempo, or more difficult.

To make a good initial choice of tempo, not in the absolute but in relation to the acoustics of the hall and the mood of the performance; to vary this tempo flexibly, yet not arbitrarily, and to return to it surely; to remember the initial choice of tempo at subsequent performances, yet adapt it to varying conditions: here is indeed a searching test of fine musicianship.

In all these ways, a good head for tempo comes from an inner gift and a practised cultivation, to which scholarship has little to contribute. There are, however, a few indications to be gleaned.

2 Baroque tempo words not consistent

Tempo words came into use very early in the baroque period, and grew plentiful in the later baroque period. They have a familiar appearance; but this is often deceptive, because time words, which never are very definite, were even more indefinite in the baroque period than they subsequently became.

Not only were tempo words employed more indefinitely in the baroque period; they were employed more inconsistently. Thus Purcell (*Sonnata's of III Parts*, London, 1683, preface) gives adagio and grave as 'very slow' and largo as a 'middle' speed; but Brossard (*Dictionaire de musique*, Paris, 1703) gives largo as 'very slow' and adagio as 'comfortably . . . dragging the speed a little'. Grassineau (*Musical Dictionary*, London, 1740) gives adagio as 'slowest of any except grave'; but a copy once owned by Dr. Burney (and now in the British Museum) has this corrected in his hand to 'the slowest of any'; while Leopold Mozart (*Violinschule*, Augsburg, 1756, I, iii, 27) gives adagio as 'slow', adagio pesante as 'somewhat slower', largo as 'still slower' and grave as 'very slow indeed'.

Can we wonder that Alexander Malcolm (*Treatise of Musick*, Edinburgh, 1721, p. 394) called tempo 'a various and undetermined thing', and time-words 'uncertain Measures', of which (p. 395) 'they leave it altogether to Practice to determine the precise Quantity' in any given piece. Leopold Mozart's comment (I, ii, 7) was that 'special words are written at the start of the piece which are supposed to give it its character, such as Allegro (lively), Adagio (slow) and so forth. But since both slow and fast have their graduations', actual tempos 'must be inferred from the music itself, and this is what infallibly shows the true quality of a musician'.

3 Dance forms not a sure guide to tempo

Dance titles are no more reliable as tempo indications than are tempo words, since these titles too are used inconsistently, and are therefore no better than a rough guide from which to start. We may take warning, for example, from the saraband, of which there was an extremely fast seventeenth-century English form, a slower Italian form, and a still slower French form later used by J. S. Bach. Mace (*Musick's Monument*, London, 1676, pp. 129ff.) gives the saraband as 'the shortest Triple-time', and 'Toyish'; Talbot (MS 1187, Christ Church, Oxford, *c.* 1690) as 'a soft passionate Movement, always set in a slow Triple'; but then, Talbot's main informants were French, and Masson's *Nouveau Traité* (2nd ed. Paris, 1699, pp. 7ff.) has 'gravely' for the saraband.

4 Baroque time-signatures in great confusion

Time-signatures were given up by Athanasius Kircher (*Musurgia*, Rome, 1650) after one of the longest and most thorough explanations of them in the baroque literature, as (p. 679) 'this utter muddle (*tota haec farrago*)'. These time-signatures, like the time-words, were used with great inconsistency, and in practice can give us very little help in choosing a good tempo.

Not even the difference between C and ₵ can be relied upon. The theory makes ₵ twice as fast as C; the practice seldom does, and Purcell (*Lessons*, London, 1696, preface) only committed himself to 'a little faster'. The theory also gives a pulse of two (rather than four) in a bar, which may then be alla breve: but Heinichen (*General-Bass*, Dresden, 1728, Pt. I, Ch. IV, Sect. 37 p. 333) remarked instructively if a little discouragingly that this, too, can be 'marked either by C or ₵'.

For reasons confusingly inherited from renaissance proportional notation, a triple time signature in early baroque music usually needs a speed very much faster than it looks to be, perhaps with breves and semibreves skipping along at a tempo we should nowadays notate by quarter notes (crotchets) and eighth notes (quavers). In early baroque music, a *change* to triple time is likely to mean a very great increase of tempo in relation to the notated values. In later baroque music, this is not nearly so likely to be the case, though there may still be some tendency in the same direction.

In any baroque music, a change of time-signature in course of the music requires much more consideration than a time-signature at the beginning. But only musicianship can decide how much adjustment, if any, is required.

5 Keeping allegros spacious and adagios on the move

As a good working rule for baroque music, *take quick movements less quickly* than might be thought; and *take slow movements less slowly* than might be thought.

'Whatever speed an Allegro demands, it ought never to depart from a controlled and reasonable movement', wrote Quantz (*Essay*, Berlin, 1752, XII, 11); 'the object must always be the feeling which is to be expressed, never only to play fast'. And C. P. E. Bach advised us (*Essay*, Berlin, 1753, III, 10) that proper attention to the 'general mood together with the fastest notes and passages included' is the way to 'prevent an allegro from being hurried and an adagio from being dragged'.

There are, of course, some allegros of which sheer speed and verve are the chief point; but in nearly every baroque allegro which is much worth playing, there is an undercurrent of seriousness only to be brought out by a certain spaciousness and breadth of performance. If the tempo is rather slower than the fastest which is practicable, there is time to phrase properly, to stretch a little here and there, to sound human rather than mechanical. The patterns can emerge, and not merely the notes. Interestingly enough, such a slightly moderated tempo may actually convey an effect of speed and brilliance better than a literally faster performance. It is possible to put so much more detail into the workmanship that there is actually more happening in a given time. Above all, there is breadth and dignity.

And conversely, there may be baroque adagios of which the tension can be increased by a tempo as slow as is practicable. It is then necessary to justify the tempo by the intensity, the suppleness, the fine nuance with which it is carried off. But even with the finest musicianship, it is very much more probable in baroque music that the intensity will not be heightened but lowered by this lingering treatment, which belongs rather to the romantic than to the baroque spirit.

78

So often we get into difficulties trying to decide just what are the best phrasing, the best bow-strokes, the best sonority and articulation for a baroque adagio, only to find that if we just move it along a little, all these problems fall into place with no more difficulty. It was not the nuancing, it was the tempo which was the real difficulty. Very seldom does a baroque adagio want a really slow tempo at all. It wants a sense of going places. We can subject it to finesse as lovingly and as subtly as we like, so long as we first make sure that it is not dragging on our hands.

The opening movement of a Handel sonata may bear the time-word 'largo'. This may strike us as a slow marking until we remember Purcell (p. 76 above) calling it a movement of 'middle' speed. There are such movements by Handel which in one manuscript are headed 'largo', in another manuscript 'adagio', and in yet another manuscript 'andante'. So little did it matter to a baroque composer or copyist what he put into the notation. He knew that the performer would decide in any event; and in such a matter, we have to act like a baroque performer and not a modern one. We have to let the music tell us what to do, and not the notation.

For modern performers, the marking 'andante' would be much more appropriate to most Handel opening movements (and others of the same kind) than 'largo' or 'adagio'. That is a piece of historical information most necessary to absorb. Moving along, going places, is almost literally the meaning of 'andante'; and that is the artistic result which brings off these movements best, as soon as we have got over the slight shock of a tempo decidedly faster than we have been brought up to apply to them.

To hold the allegros back and to keep the adagios moving is the most effective general principle for choosing a good tempo in baroque music.

6 Tempo changes in baroque music

Whenever the mood changes within a baroque movement, in such a way as to suggest a change of tempo, that change should be made without waiting for any written indication in the notation. It was expected of the baroque performer, and is desirable for us.

'Now slowly, now quickly', wrote Girolamo Frescobaldi of his own toccatas (*Toccate*, Rome, 1615–16, preface, Section 1), 'to match the expressive effects'; for (9) 'it is left to the good taste and fine judgement of the performer to regulate the tempo'. Thomas Mace (*Musick's Monument*, London, 1676, p. 81) wanted us to '*Break Time; sometimes Faster, and sometimes Slower*', with some sections or passages taken 'very *Briskly, and Couragiously*', others '*Gently, Lovingly, Tenderly, and Smoothly*'. And as an example of such change of tempo within a movement, without written indication in the notation, but for reasons of expression, C. P. E. Bach suggested (*Essay*, Berlin, I, 1753, [4th] ed., Leipzig, 1787, III, 28) that 'Passages in music in the major mode which are repeated in the minor way may be taken somewhat more slowly in this repetition, because of the expression.' Sets of variations are particularly liable to need changes of tempo in response to changes of mood, without written indication.

7 Rallentandos in baroque music

Rallentandos can best be judged by the feeling of the harmony. As soon as the harmony suggests a definitely cadential tendency (and this happens very often in baroque music) the question arises whether to stretch the tempo in response. This cannot be done all the time, or the music would fall to pieces. But it can be done more frequently and more flexibly than is often supposed.

The stretching of the tempo may usually be so slight that no one in the audience actually notices a rallentando; the audience merely experiences a sense of natural ease and relaxation, because stiffness and remorselessness have been gracefully avoided.

When the cadence has rather more importance in the structure of the piece, the rallentando may be appreciable although not necessarily con-spicuous. When the cadence concludes a distinct portion of the movement (for example, the opening exposition of an ordinary baroque allegro), then the rallentando must be conspicuous enough to draw proper attention to the fact. When the movement is coming to its final cadence, the rallentando must reduce the momentum early enough, or steeply enough, or both in due proportion, so that the audience feels satisfied without questioning why or how. Provided that the rallentando is begun and graded in response to the harmony, as this takes on the unmistakable cadential flavour, it will not sound arbitrary or excessive. There is nothing unbaroque about a big rallen-tando if it fits the progression of the harmony.

No rallentando at all (senza ritardando) is a special effect, and a flashy one. Just occasionally it may make a startling impression, but it is much too gimmicky for anything but the rarest possible use.

Girolamo Frescobaldi may instruct us again in his early baroque adven-turousness (*Toccate*, Rome, 1615–16, preface, Section 5): 'The cadences, although they may be written quickly, are properly to be very much drawn out; and in approaching the end of passages or cadences, one proceeds by drawing out the time more adagio.' Jean Rousseau wrote in his *Traité de la Viole* (Paris, 1687, p. 60) that such 'liberties may be taken'; and François Couperin (*L'art de toucher le clavecin*, Paris, 1716, ed. of 1717, p. 38) called them 'the spirit, the soul that must be added' to the strict 'measure' of the music.

8 Flexibility the life of baroque tempo

We meet here the most general principle of baroque expression: flexibility. Joachim Quantz summed it up (*Essay*, Berlin, 1752, XI, 13): 'The performance should be easy and flexible . . . without stiffness and constraint.'

CHAPTER XIII

Rhythm in Baroque Music

1 A good head for rhythm

Rhythm, like tempo, is one of those elements of musical expression which depend on natural talent and practised cultivation. Historical knowledge of the baroque methods is quite secondary to that. However, there is more assistance to be had from a knowledge of the baroque conventions with regard to rhythm than there is with regard to tempo.

A fuller discussion will be found in my *Performer's Guide to Baroque Music* (London, 1973). The following may serve to introduce the subject for most purposes of baroque fiddling.

2 Baroque inequality

Inequality is a term for that baroque (and subsequent) convention by which *notes which are written equally may be performed unequally*.

This is 'because the inequality gives them more grace', Michel de Saint-Lambert explained in his *Principes du Clavecin* (Paris, 1702, p. 25); but 'taste judges of this as it does of tempo'. And indeed it is important to be aware that there are only certain limited situations in which inequality can be justified historically or made to sound satisfactory artistically.

(i) *Inequality only applies to notes which are grouped or groupable by pairs*

(a) When notes are *slurred by pairs* as written in the notation, or can be successfully slurred by pairs in the performance, inequality may be possible.

(b) When notes are slurred by threes, fours or any other number in notation or performance, inequality is not possible.

(ii) *Inequality chiefly applies to notes which are paired by step*

(a) When the notes thus paired *join each other mainly by step*, inequality

82

may be probable (it does not matter whether the *pairs* are *separated* from each other by step or by leap).

(b) When the notes thus paired *join each other mainly by leap*, inequality is most improbable, with exceptions such as the not very typical variety described in iv(a) below.

MUSIC EXAMPLE B

(iii) *Inequality applies in principle to the shortest notes*

In principle, inequality applies, if at all, to *the shortest notes* appearing in substantial numbers during the piece or passage.

When these shortest notes are so fast that to take them unequally would sound too agitated or too skittish, then inequality is precluded, both on historical and artistic grounds. Inequality does not generally go with fast movements at all.

When the shortest notes are so slow that to take them unequally would sound too ponderous or too forced, then inequality is likewise precluded. Inequality generally goes with moderate to slow movements, but within beats or sub-beats rather than between beats. A sluggish inequality is undesirable.

When the shortest notes do not appear in substantial numbers, then: (a) if these shortest notes are either very fast or fairly fast, they can be ignored for the purposes of this rule, leaving the next shortest notes liable to inequality; or (b) alternatively, if the shortest notes are fairly fast but not very fast, both these shortest notes, and the next to shortest notes, can (where otherwise suitable) be taken unequally.

MUSIC EXAMPLE C

(iv) *Inequality may be vigorous or lilting*

(a) In a vigorous piece or passage, *inequality should itself be vigorous:*

the effect is to increase the energy of the performance. The degree of inequality may be the equivalent of dotting or a little more.

Not only stepwise pairs but leaping pairs are liable to vigorous inequality if otherwise suitable. But in practice this situation does not often arise, because most pieces of a kind to require it have sufficient unequalness already written into the notation as dotted notes.

(b) In a lilting piece or passage, *inequality should itself be lilting*: the effect is to increase the gracefulness of the performance. The degree of inequality may be more or less the equivalent of triplet rhythm.

Only pairs which are mainly stepwise are ordinarily liable to lilting inequality. But in practice this is a situation which very often arises, because at all times and places during the baroque period (not only, as has been misinferred by some modern specialists, in France), this graceful convention was a very familiar option for the performer.

(v) *Inequality may be standard or reversed*

(a) The standard direction in which inequality may modify the rhythm is *forwards*: the first note of each pair is lengthened as desired; the second note is proportionately shortened. The effect, in the proper contexts, sounds natural, whether as vigorous inequality or as lilting inequality.

(b) The reversed direction in which inequality may modify the rhythm is *backwards*: the first note of each pair is shortened as desired; the second note is proportionately lengthened. The effect, even in the proper contexts, is not so much natural as conspicuous.

Thus standard inequality is a normal effect, which can be used very commonly and freely in the proper contexts. But reversed inequality (in the rhythm sometimes known as Lombard rhythm, and sometimes as the Scotch snap) is a special effect, which can be excellent in a proper context, but is under no circumstances to be used very commonly or freely.

(vi) *Inequality is optional, but not arbitrary*

There are many baroque and some post-baroque pieces and passages in which inequality is so strongly implied that most baroque performers would probably have used it, and we may well wish to do the same. Nevertheless, there can never be any obligation to do so; for *inequality is essentially a performer's option*.

The inequality most likely to be implied so strongly as this is lilting inequality on mainly stepwise pairs of notes in andante or adagio: particularly in simple triple time, which when given lilting inequality (in approximately triplet rhythm) may in approximate effect be turned into compound triple time; and it can even, if so desired, be written out thus by the editor (e.g. as nine-eight in place of three-four) so as to save time and avoid confusion in rehearsal.

In the vast majority of ordinary baroque allegros, inequality of any variety is likely to be quite out of place. If, for example, vigorous inequality is used to give a dotted rhythm to passages written with equal notes or mainly so, the effect, particularly if the passage has more leaps than steps, is merely to turn an easy flow into a jerky uneasiness. Nothing so unnatural can be justified historically or accepted artistically.

And even in a baroque andante or adagio, where lilting inequality may most suitably introduce a triplet gracefulness, this can sometimes sound too sophisticated when the music itself is essentially rather simple; and again, there are some movements, for example a typical Italian andante with a striding bass in equal eighth notes (quavers), in which inequality of any variety is definitely precluded, on both historical and artistic grounds.

Inequality, therefore, although it can under no circumstances be obligatory for the performer, is not free to the performer's option. It has its proper contexts, and its proper uses in those contexts. Inequality of rhythm, as introduced by the performer in baroque music, is an attractive but not an arbitrary possibility.

3 Baroque dotted notes

In baroque (and slightly subsequent) convention, notes written dotted are not (as now) necessarily half as long again, but may be varied either for expression, or for mere convenience. This is *variable dotting*.

When a dotted note is set against other moving notes, its length may be (though it is not always) determined as an exact fit.

When a dotted note is not set against other moving notes (and sometimes even when it is), its length may not be determined as an exact fit. It is then variable at the performer's option.

Whether as an exact fit or as free expression, the length of the baroque dot may be variable as follows.

(i) *A baroque dot may extend to less than the standard length*

We may need or wish to take the dotted note for less than half as long again, and lengthen proportionately the note or notes which follow it: this is *under-dotting*.

The effect of under-dotting is to soften off a rhythm, written dotted, more or less to triplet rhythm in performance. Thus notes written dotted may be reduced, by under-dotting, to the same degree of unequalness to which notes written equal may be raised by lilting inequality.

Under-dotting may be for expression, as for example in many extensive passages of Purcell where the notation goes on being dotted but the performance sounds much more natural and beautiful if softened off more or less to triplet rhythm.

Or under-dotting may be for convenience, as when one part is written in dotted notes against another part written in triplets (or in compound triple time). Here the dotted notes can usually (though not always) be best taken under-dotted. This assimilates the dotted rhythm to the triplet rhythm, and is a mere instance of inexact baroque notation which the performer was expected to take correctly on his own initiative (but not every case falls under this simple rule).

(ii) *A baroque dot may extend to standard length*

We may, and most commonly shall, take the dotted note for half as long again, and the note or notes which follow it at written length: this is *standard dotting*.

But even standard dotting is hardly ever mathematically exact, in baroque or any other music, except in so far as other parts moving against it require it to be exact.

(iii) *A baroque dot may extend to more than the standard length*

We may need or wish to take the dotted note for more than half as long again, and shorten proportionately the note or notes which follow it: this is *over-dotting*.

The effect of over-dotting is to sharpen up a rhythm, written dotted, to almost or exactly or more than double-dotted.

Over-dotting may be for expression, as when a brisk and march-like motion is made yet more brisk and march-like by this very obvious and common crispening. The French Overture (and music related to it) is a very important instance for baroque (and somewhat subsequent) interpretation. The overture to Handel's *Messiah* is a good case in point; and J. S. Bach's B minor French Overture is another (compare the conventional misnotation of the C minor version with the correct notation of the B minor version; both are meant to be performed the same, i.e. approximately at notated in the B minor version).

Or over-dotting likewise may be for convenience, as when a note written dotted requires more length merely to fill out the value required of it by the note or notes which follow: another instance of inexact baroque notation which a baroque performer would have unhesitatingly corrected (and we must do the same).

MUSIC EXAMPLE D
Notated (standard):   Underdotted: Overdotted: Or:

Handel, sonata in A min. for flute, oboe or violin, Larghetto
As notated for convenience: As intended:

4 Baroque fluidity of rhythm

As with tempo, so with rhythm: it is not baroque to be mathematical; it is baroque to be flexible.

It is not necessary to maintain an undeviating consistency of rhythm from one end of a piece to the other. If a rather greater or lesser inequality, a rather gentler or sharper dotting suits one part of a piece than suits another, then a certain tactful adaptation is in order, provided that the shape of things carries conviction as a whole.

Things which really are the same should be shaped the same; but the same figure in a new counterpoint or with new harmonies may not be altogether the same thing, and it is here that it may actually be a virtue to keep the rhythmic patterns, like the tempos, a little on the fluid side.

CHAPTER XIV

Shape in Baroque Music

1 Phrasing and dynamics as shaping factors

In baroque music, the line is the thing. Unless the line is well sustained wherever it wants sustaining, and well divided wherever it wants dividing, the music degenerates into confusion, fragmentary or indistinct as the case may be, and earth-bound in either case. For baroque music to get airborne, it is above all the line which has to soar and glow.

(a) The flow of sound has first of all to be reliably there: that means good dynamic control, so that nothing falls back or stands out unintentionally. For a singer, it is a matter of breath-control: for a violinist, it is a matter of bow-control; and the effect is very similar. There is a flawless arch of sound, patterned and nuanced only by intentional design.

(b) But this intentional patterning and nuancing is the second requirement: for this, phrasing and articulation provide the patterning; dynamics and accentuation provide the nuancing.

Together (and in combination with the proper rallentandos as described on p. 80), these factors give the music shape.

2 Baroque phrasing

Phrases generally go to a peak note, which is often though not always the highest note, and then relax to a note given away at the end. There is the unit: that much, and no less nor more, is the phrase; and it is for our own musicianship to recognize the fact. Nothing in the notation, and nothing in the historical evidence, is going to show us the pattern if our own musicianship does not. Good modern performers often understand the shapes and divisions of the baroque phrases very well; but they do not always have the courage of their convictions in making these shapes and divisions sufficiently evident to the audience.

88

'A pause', wrote Girolamo Frescobaldi (*Toccate*, Rome, 1615–16, preface, Sect. 4), 'prevents confusion between one phrase and another'. Thomas Mace (*Musick's Monument*, London, 1676, p. 109), called it 'a kind of *Cessation*, or *standing still*, sometimes *Longer*, and sometimes *Shorter*, according to the Nature, or Requiring . . . of the musick'.

François Couperin, in the preface to his *Troisième Livre de Pièces* (Paris, 1722) also wrote of these 'silences' of phrasing, which he himself sometimes (and very untypically) marked with a comma sign. Joachim Quantz (*Essay*, Berlin, 1752, VII, 4, French version) wanted phrases to be 'well separated and distinguished from one another'.

(a) There may be a silence taken out of the time of the note before, so that the sound is interrupted but not the tempo (*articulated time*): or

(b) there may be a silence inserted after the note before, and added to the time-value, so that the tempo is interrupted as well as the sound (*stolen time*).

Both forms may be varied in length; both should commonly be quite long and conspicuous; but the second is inherently more conspicuous than the first.

There is an art of *placing* a note or a phrase with just such a degree of separation or actual delay that it sounds exactly right and perfectly punctual, though in fact it is later than the literal measure would require. The effect is not of being unpunctual, but of being spacious. To be literally punctual would not sound wrong; but it would sound perfunctory.

Half the secret of good baroque phrasing is to space it out with breadth and poise and a fine sense of drama. The timing is as important as an actor's timing in the theatre; and he is never afraid to keep his audience suspended until the tension is perfectly prepared. Then his next entry comes with the utmost impact; and so it is with well-placed phrasing in baroque music. The art is to keep the audience waiting for it, not too long, but just long enough.

Slow movements naturally leave more space for silences of phrasing than fast movements; but fast movements are more apt to have their silences of phrasing overlooked; or if not overlooked, then performed with too little distinctness to reach the audience sufficiently. In particular, an ordinary baroque allegro with long passages of sixteenth notes (semiquavers) will sound dull, mechanical and a little pointless unless these passages are broken down into their constituent phrases with a distinctness which may even appear exaggerated to the performer, yet which may reach the audience as a perfectly natural but clear succession of phrases.

As a mere string of notes all alike, such a passage can have very little meaning or interest. But as a pattern built up out of brief but completed phrases, separated by unmistakable silences with or without an instant of stolen time, that same string of notes will come to life and grip the audience.

There will be excitement, not merely speed; and if a slightly slower tempo is desirable to give time for this distinctive phrasing, there may nevertheless be a greater impression of speed than at a mere under-phrased rush.

Distinctive phrasing is the foundation on which good shaping for a baroque movement has to stand.

3 Baroque articulation

We have already considered (on pp. 15–16 above) the effect on articulation of the baroque bow and the modern bow; and (in Ch. VI–IX above) the effect on articulation of the many different bow strokes properly available for baroque fiddling.

All degrees of articulateness, from the smoothest legato up to the hardest staccato, have some place in baroque music, except probably a heavy marcato such as the hammered stroke (martelé) produces (particularly at the heel); and the placing of a single note has sometimes to be as purposefully delayed, as unpunctually punctual, as the placing of a complete new phrase.

It is not always necessary or desirable to keep to an identical articulation throughout a passage. It is more often desirable to nuance the articulation with much subtle variation, so that it contributes not only to the character of a phrase, but to its melodic shape.

One important instance of this principle concerns bass parts, which frequently need as much melodic shaping as the upper parts. Where, for example, the bass line has a succession of moderate or short notes mainly the same in length, we should modify the articulation, within the general character, so that no two successive notes are quite the same; and the peak note, in particular, may be given an agogic accent by lingering on it a fraction longer than on the others. For bass parts, too, need patterning into phrases, and their phrases have peak notes, to which they rise and from which they fall away, just as upper melodies may do. Subtle nuances of articulation contribute to the shaping of any melody, in any part.

But the general character of the articulation in most baroque allegros should be quite crisp and distinct; for the standard articulation is not legato, though it is not staccato either. It is midway between legato and staccato.

Baroque slow movements may in general need the smoothest sort of cantabile (though always distinctively phrased). Yet even within the smooth cantabile which gives the general character, there can be gradations of articulateness which give the detailed moulding. These gradations are produced and largely inspired by subtleties of bowing such as all good fiddlers know how to cultivate.

4 Baroque dynamics

Dynamic markings occur from the start of the baroque period, and increasingly towards its end. But at no time do baroque expression marks attempt a full indication for baroque expression. We can best regard them as hints, as did the baroque performers themselves, and use our own judgement and initiative, as they did. When anything approaching a full complement of dynamic or other expression marks does occur in an edition of baroque music, we may safely assume that many or all of them have only been put in by the modern editor, and are not to be found in any of the original sources. If the editor is scholarly, he will have distinguished his own markings from any original markings; but we cannot count on it. We do not *have* to follow an editor.

We may distinguish two different, although overlapping, varieties of dynamic expression.

(i) *Dynamic contrasts may be used for structural shaping*

It is important to work out, for a baroque movement, a broad scheme of louds and softs which will make the *structure* both clear and interesting.

For example, an ordinary baroque allegro may present its opening material in an exposition of some considerable length and boldness, followed by a much more quiet and contemplative development, with farther ranging modulations, but leading at last to a decisive restatement of the opening material, as boldly as before, and this time conclusively. Such a structure invites a loud opening, a soft development and a loud conclusion. The sudden return to forte (with or without a brief crescendo, but certainly with a sufficient rallentando, leading up to it) makes the return to the opening mood far more clear, and far more dramatic, than if we fall into the temptation of some premature forte before this crucial point in the structure arrives.

This is only by way of example, since structures are not all the same; but it can be an extremely effective example of using the simplest means to the most telling effects. A soft beginning to a baroque allegro, marked and intended piano, would be a very rare effect. A forte beginning would not be marked: it would be taken for granted. To begin a baroque slow movement piano (or mezzo-piano, because of the need to catch sufficient attention at the beginning of a movement) is much commoner and much more likely to be effectual.

The principle here is to find out the basic structure of the piece (not always so simple, of course, as has been described above); and then to work out the simplest overall scheme of louds and softs which will make it clear and interesting to the audience, resisting all temptations to be too clever or to make striking effects merely for their own sake. The structure is what the overall dynamic scheme is there to serve.

A brief echo effect (the same or similar bars played forte and repeated piano) may be built into the structure of some baroque movements, and sometimes marked, particularly at the end of Italian allegros; again, the structure is both the indication and the object of the operation.

'We play Loud or Soft' wrote Christopher Simpson in his *Division-Violist* (London, 1659, 2nd ed. 1665 and 1667, p. 10), 'according to our fancy, or the humour [character] of the music'; and 'this interchange of soft and loud', Joachim Quantz insisted in his *Essay* (Berlin, 1752, XII, 23, French version), 'gives much grace to the performance'. It also gives much clarity to the structure.

(ii) *Dynamic contrasts may be used for textural moulding*

Besides making the structure of the music clear and interesting, dynamic contrasts make the *texture* lively and expressive.

Thus in the example of a simple baroque allegro given above, within each portion broadly kept on one dynamic level, there would need to be introduced finer dynamic gradations; but whereas the structural dynamics can best be worked out, and at least pencilled into the players' parts, the textural dynamics can never be finalized, and should probably not be written down, since that might lead to performing them too rigidly and too conspicuously.

'Learn to fill, and soften a sound, as shades in needlework', Roger North recommended in his own autobiographical notes around 1695 (ed. Jessopp, London, 1887, Sect. 106); and Joachim Quantz in his *Essay* (Berlin, 1752, XI, 14) again confirmed that 'light and shade must be continuously introduced'.

It was the nature both of the harpsichord and of the organ, as the baroque period developed and valued these noble instruments, *not* to introduce dynamic 'light and shade' as passing nuances, but only as decisive contrasts between often quite lengthy portions of the music (so-called 'terrace dynamics'). This makes passing nuances of phrasing and articulation all the more important; and the result can be just as expressive in its own solid way. But the voice, the violin and most other baroque instruments are as well fitted by nature for dynamic shadings as the baroque harpsichord and organ are unfitted. Our baroque fiddling would be incomplete indeed if it did not employ every appropriate crescendo and diminuendo, every means 'to fill, and soften a sound' or a whole passage, which comes naturally to this most flexible family of instruments.

One particular manner in which the dynamic nuancing may clarify the texture (and indirectly, the structure) is by attending to the balance. This is most important when the texture is in any degree contrapuntal. 'Entries should be emphasized a little', wrote the famous Zacconi, at the threshold of the baroque period, in his *Prattica di musica* (Venice, 1592, LXVI, p. 59), 'so as to be instantly and clearly recognized by the hearer': a very proper line of argument.

Whether in counterpoint or not, 'a distinctive manner of performance' was required by Joachim Quantz (*Essay*, Berlin, 1752, XII, 23) for bringing out the subject, 'as well as by loud and soft'. Charles Avison (*Essay on Musical Expression*, London, 1752, p. 128) asked that 'when the inner Parts are intended as Accompanyments only' they 'may never predominate, but be always subservient to the principal Performer, who also should observe the same Method, whenever his Part becomes an Accompanyment', so that 'every Performer' has to be 'listening to the other Parts, without which he cannot do Justice to his own'.

5 Baroque accentuation

Dots or wedges or dashes, under or over notes, sometimes indicate degrees of accentuation in baroque sources; but we are much more often left in the usual way to decide the matter for ourselves. It is to be noticed that the appearance of any of these signs or of words such as staccato, marqué, détaché or détachez etc., precludes the use of inequality (for which see p. 82f.).

The practicable varieties of baroque accentuation on string instruments have been discussed in connection with the bowing techniques which produce them (for which see pp. 54–56).

The effect of a dynamic accent can be greatly increased on any instrument capable of making an accent of this kind (and can be suggested on instruments, such as the harpsichord and the organ, scarcely capable of it) by leaving a silence of articulation before the note accented. This silence will usually be taken out of the time of the note before, but may sometimes be inserted as a moment of stolen time (for which see p. 89), both in fast movements and in slow.

Accentuation has structural consequences in so far as it helps to establish the peak notes (often but not always the highest notes) of phrases. Accents may also have consequences for the texture in bringing out fugal entries or other significant subjects, and in combining with the articulation to give a characteristic texture to whole passages.

A special effect of *displaced* accentuation occurs in the hemiola (or hemiolia). Two bars of triple time (*one* two three, *one* two three) are accented as if they were one bar of twice the length (*one* two, *three* one, *two* three), the bar-line in between being deleted (e.g. two three-four bars can be beaten as one three-two bar). To spot a hemiola, notice on which beats the bass carries a change of harmony; if the second 'one' has no change of harmony, a hemiola is indicated. Perform it unmistakably, suppressing the bar-line in the middle as if it did not exist, and accenting the alternate beats strongly to bring out the pattern (Music Ex. E).

MUSIC EXAMPLE E
Handel, Trio Sonata in G min., Op. II, No. 8, last movement, hemiola rhythm

CHAPTER XV

Ornamenting Baroque Music

1 Ornamentation and ornaments

The object of ornamenting music is to bring in an element of joyful spontaneity, by which the performer can express his exuberance and his fantasy over and beyond whatever the composer has already imagined.

By the baroque period, composers had by and large taken over from performers the responsibility for the structure itself. But a great deal of the ornamental figuration of that structure remained (like the expression) with the performer. In fast movements he might alter it at will; in slow movements he had often to provide it altogether, since merely the outlines of the melody are sketched by the composer into the written notation. All this can be called *ornamentation*.

In course of the baroque period, there crystallized within this ancient tradition of free ornamentation many small ornamental formulas, also left with the performer in the main (though signs for some of them do occur, and a few of them were subject to accepted conventions amounting virtually to obligations). These can be called *ornaments*.

2 Free ornamentation in baroque music

There can be no obligation to introduce a particular ornamentation, but only to introduce enough ornamentation for any passage which implies such ornamentation, and which therefore sounds bald and unconvincing if performed merely as notated. At certain points, either indicated by a fermata or (probably) left to the performer to spot, a *cadenza* is implied. Any suitable cadenza will do it; but there should be a cadenza.

One late baroque situation implying some suitable ornamentation is the da capo repeats of big arias, to give them the novelty of some (but not too much) fresh figuration. One or more cadenzas may also be implied, for example at the end of the middle, and especially at the end of the da capo repeat.

For violinists, the baroque situation most clearly implying some suitable ornamentation is a slow movement in Italianate solo or trio sonatas. Here fresh figuration, by the editor or by each performer at will, is needed where little or no figuration may appear in the original, but only the bare skeleton of structural notes on which to hang it.

Fast movements will normally have enough figuration provided by the composer in the notation (with a few exceptions such as the need to improvise interesting arpeggiation on chords notated plain for the purpose). Nevertheless, baroque virtuosi habitually modified or supplanted the composer's figuration with different figuration of their own, and the modern performer is entitled to do the same if he so desires.

Cadenzas are often needed, usually on the dominant harmony before an important or final cadence; and it is important to spot these points of expectancy and respond to the need, since otherwise there will be a lack of proper balance and completeness. Many of these cadenzas should be very short, and others of moderate length. Quantz wrote (*Essay*, Berlin, 1752, XV, 17) that whereas cadenzas for voices or wind instruments should be 'within one breath', and whereas 'a string player can make them as long as he likes', they will nevertheless make a much better effect 'through a reasonable shortness than through a tiresome length'. There is no place in baroque music for the very long cadenzas expected in classical concertos, where they serve a more structural purpose than the baroque cadenza.

The harmony on which a baroque cadenza falls may be the customary dominant six-four of the classical cadenza, though not so insistently presented, and more probably before the final close rather than before the closing section. Or the written harmony may be a mere dominant five-three; but in that case, the cadenza may reach a six-four as the normal upper-note start of the cadential trill with which it should conclude.

Whatever the ornamentation, it should be added or supplemented with moderation; it should be musically related to what is there already; and it should be performed with verve and lightness. Extravagant or incongruous ornamentation is not unhistorical, since we know from contemporary complaints that it all too often happened. But it is inartistic; and the proper precaution against that is to avoid so covering the original melody that it can no longer be heard and enjoyed for its own sake.

3 Specific ornaments in baroque music

Baroque violinists were not expected to know the very numerous, confusing and inconsistent signs which harpsichordists, organists and to some extent singers and lutanists affected. A simple + or × sufficed for a variety of common ornaments, especially the trill, for which t or tr were also used. Modern violinists have no need to burden themselves unduly with the signs, which are thoroughly unreliable, nor with the names, which are often no less so. Violinists interested in the chamber music of François Couperin and a few other French composers should pay exceptional attention to the signs there, because these composers took care over their ornaments and used signs for them consistently and clearly enough to be taken seriously.

The regular ornaments of which violinists need some practical knowledge for baroque music are: the appoggiatura; the slide; the trill; the mordent; the turn; the double cadence.

(i) *The appoggiatura is generally long and always on the beat*

(a) *The short appoggiatura* is a genuine though not typical appoggiatura, taken on the beat but not absorbing any considerable part of it. The notation, if any, may be by a cue-size note (but *not* with a stroke across its tail or tails, which modern editors use but baroque composers did not in this meaning). Take no notice of its apparent value, but just make it brief, unmeasured and usually rather well accented.

The chief difficulty is to know when to use a short appoggiatura. Certainly on a main note which itself is short; sometimes to fill in descending thirds, or on main notes repeated at the same pitch; occasionally on longer notes where the harmony will not accept a long appoggiatura (but with ornaments it is surprising what rough progressions, as they look on paper, will sound absolutely right, as heard by the ear).

(b) *The long appoggiatura* is a typical appoggiatura, far more frequent and important than the short appoggiatura. The long appoggiatura is also taken on the beat, but absorbs at least half of it and very often more. Take no notice of the apparent value of any cue-size notation shown, but lean lovingly on the appoggiatura; hold it as long as the context allows; and resolve the discord usually resulting, by passing to the main note with that slight decrease in volume which resolutions ordinarily require.

The standard rules for long appoggiaturas give the following lengths: on duple notes, half the value; on dotted notes, two-thirds of the value; and on dotted notes tied over to a following note, all the dotted note. Rather long notes may not always need an appoggiatura so long in proportion. Rather short notes usually need their (relatively) long appoggiaturas according to the rule. Except on very short notes, the long appoggiatura is much more probable than the short appoggiatura, and should be tried first. There is no need to be put off by a considerable degree of harshness or even (theoretical) incorrectness in the progressions which may result; but conspicuously incorrect consecutives are perhaps best avoided.

(c) The so-called *passing appoggiatura* is not a genuine appoggiatura, being taken as an unaccented passing note between beats. It is fairly common in some French baroque music; rare elsewhere; and nowhere of an importance comparable to the genuine appoggiatura, long or short, from which its notation (if any) may, unfortunately, be indistinguishable (Music Ex. F).

MUSIC EXAMPLE F
Quantz, Tab. VI, suggested lengths for appoggiaturas:

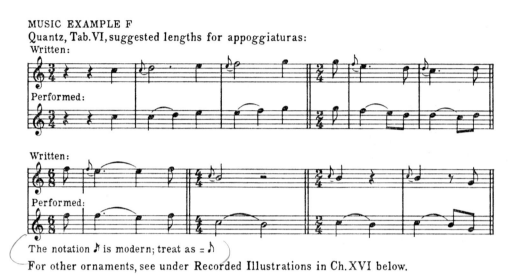

The notation ♪ is modern; treat as = ♪

For other ornaments, see under Recorded Illustrations in Ch. XVI below.

(ii) *The slide is best taken accented on the beat*

The *slide* is a little run of three notes (usually up but sometimes down) filling in a melodic third. Almost all baroque authorities show it accented on the beat, which is the best and strongest interpretation. The slide can be taken more rapidly for a vigorous passage, more lingeringly for an expressive passage, but in either case unmeasured, so that it sounds like an ornament. The most typical slides are quite well accented and quite fast: none are very slow.

(iii) *The baroque trill starts with its upper note, accented on the beat*

The *trill* can be a purely melodic ornament, starting with the upper or the lower note, though in fact every regular baroque table of ornaments shows the upper-note start, and on the beat.

The baroque trill, however, came to be a primarily harmonic ornament. In this form, the trill has to start from the upper note, on the beat, well accented and often more or less prolonged; for it is this upper note which affects the harmony.

(a) By far the most important baroque trill is the *cadential trill*. It is this ornament which Pier Francesco Tosi in his *Opinioni* (Bologna, 1723, transl. J. E. Galliard, London, 1742, p. 42) called 'very essential', and which Joachim

Quantz, in his *Essay* (Berlin, 1752, IX, i) called 'indispensably necessary' because it is the normal way of approaching a substantial cadence. Whether any sign for it, or none, is shown in the written notation, it was expected, and it is in effect really quite obligatory.

Countless baroque cadences are written as plain progressions of dominant five-three harmony to tonic five-three harmony. The cadential trill enlivens them by changing the harmony. When the dominant third is trilled, its upper note is the fourth, which (being well accented, on the beat, and more or less prolonged) introduces an unwritten dominant five-four. This resolves through dominant five-three (the bottom note of the trill), to tonic five-three (or a delayed cadence). Or if the dominant fifth is trilled, its upper note is the sixth, which introduces an unwritten dominant six-three resolving through dominant five-three to tonic five-three. Or if both the third and the fifth are trilled (i.e. in thirds or sixths or tenths together), their upper notes are the fourth and the sixth, which introduces an unwritten dominant six-four resolving through dominant five-three to tonic five-three.

These considerations will make it obvious why the cadential trill must not only start on the beat with its upper note, but also have that upper note really well accented, and at least to some extent prolonged before the repercussions of the trill (which provide the resolution) begin. It is useless to start with the upper note before the beat, unaccented; and it is almost useless to start with the upper note on the beat, but unaccented. The whole accentuation of the trill has got to go from the upper note to the lower, both at the start and throughout the repercussions.

(b) The repercussions of the trill normally proceed at an even speed: neither so fast as to sound like a goat bleating (*chevroté* was the baroque word for it); or so slow as to sound (dare I add?) like a donkey braying. Quick movements may tolerate faster trills than slow movements. Slow movements may occasionally tolerate a slightly accelerating trill. But steady repercussions are normal and usually best.

Full trills *must be terminated*, whether so shown in the written notation or not. The turned ending is the most versatile, and will do almost anywhere: its normal behaviour (even when misleadingly notated as slower notes) is to be joined *without break* to the trill, of which it simply sounds like the last repercussion. The ending by a little note of anticipation (i.e. anticipating the ensuing tonic) is not much less versatile, and in very many cases is an equally acceptable termination, whether written into the notation or not. But if written, it may likewise be written misleadingly, as much longer (and by implication heavier) than it is meant to be performed. Take it short, and take it light, just slipped in easily at the last possible moment: either separated from its trill by a silence of articulation, for more vigour; or slurred with its trill, for more smoothness.

(c) If no termination is desired, do not use a full trill (which must be terminated), but a *half-trill* (which should not be terminated). The half-trill begins with its upper note accented on the beat, like the full trill; but there are only two repercussions (four notes) or at most three repercussions (six notes). The rest of the value is filled in by staying on the main note.

The speed of the half-trill should not be slow, but may be moderate or fast. When very fast on a descending step (a favourable position for this ornament) the half-trill may lose its first (upper) note purely as an effect of the speed; it then becomes an inverted (upper) mordent, otherwise not used in the main baroque period.

(d) 'All shakes [trills] are taken from the note above', we read unequivocally in the 'Rules for Gracing', i.e. ornamenting, which an anonymous contemporary wrote out, in a seventeenth-century hand, on the reverse of page 67 of his copy (now at the Royal College of Music in London) of Christopher Simpson's *Division-Violist* (London, 1659).

(iv) *The baroque mordent goes not up but down*

The baroque mordent is an opposite of the half-trill. Its most favourable positions are (a) on an ascending step (but *not* a descending step, because then the ornament weakly anticipates the ensuing note, whereas the half-trill weakly anticipates the ensuing note on an ascending step); (b) on the top note of a leap, especially (although not only) in the bass.

The baroque mordent (*standard mordent*) always goes from the main note to the note below, and back again; never to the note above (*inverted mordent*) except, in practice, as a half-trill curtailed of its first note by the effect of high speed, for which see Sect. iii (c) on p. 100 above. There is usually one repercussion (two notes), but more are possible. The speed is usually fast and the effect vigorous, but slower and more lingering mordents are possible in expressive passages. The interval is usually diatonic, but may also be chromatic, whether so shown in the written notation or (more often) not.

(v) *The baroque turn is unrestricted in its behaviour*

The baroque turn may be (a) accented on the beat (*accented turn*) or (b) unaccented between beats (*unaccented turn*). The unaccented turn is the more common. The baroque turn may start (a) on the note above the main note (*standard* or *upper turn*) or (b) on the note below the main note (*inverted* or *lower turn*). The standard turn is much the more common. The speed of the baroque turn ranges from fairly slow to moderately fast: moderate is the most common.

(vi) *The baroque double cadence a compound ornament*

The *double cadence* is among a type of baroque ornament arising when two or more single ornaments are joined continuously to form a *compound ornament.*

One rather expressive double cadence comprises two trills, the first on written six-four harmony (into which it introduces an unwritten seven), the second on written five-three harmony (into which it introduces an unwritten six), both on the same dominant bass. Another very useful double cadence is an unaccented standard turn on the first half of the same dominant bass, and a normal cadential trill on the second half. The name double cadence was also sometimes given to a trill prefixed by a slide (*ascending trill*) or by a standard turn (*descending trill*).

These and many other ornaments are described and illustrated in my long book, *The Interpretation of Early Music*, New Version (London, 1974) and less extensively in my shorter book, *A Performer's Guide to Baroque Music* (London, 1973). Both these books are attempts of mine to explore the wider possibilities of baroque interpretation, and are suggested reading for performers who wish to follow up further some of the many topics here introduced.

PART FOUR
The Recorded
Illustrations

CHAPTER XVI

The Illustrations Explained

1 A working sample for ordinary use

String playing for baroque music requires two general qualities, which have been described in this book together with some technical methods directed towards obtaining them. They are: a transparent sonority; and a crisp articulation. The recorded illustrations offer a working sample of these general qualities, which are more important to good baroque performance than any detail.

With the instruments and bows in ordinary present use, we shall not get quite the historical baroque sounds. But we can get sounds which match up with baroque music artistically; and this will be the aim of most though not all performers interested now in improving their baroque performances. The recorded illustrations demonstrate nothing which cannot be sufficiently carried out under these ordinary modern conditions: i.e. with instrument and bow as normally used today.

Yehudi Menuhin used his Stradivarius violin which is dated 1714, but which was fitted in the ordinary modern manner, and strung with steel wire E, aluminium-covered gut-cored A and D, silver-covered gut-cored G: perhaps the commonest and certainly the most satisfactory choice of ordinary modern stringing. As a control sample, Menuhin recorded one passage on his Guanerius violin made in 1739, also fitted in the ordinary modern manner, but strung with gut E, A and D, and silver-covered gut-cored G: a baroque stringing, and no longer ordinary, although it was so well into the early years of this century. This is an expedient which can easily be tried, and the tangy sound of the plain gut, especially from the gut E, is decidedly individual and enjoyable. The gut E is more glittering; the gut A and the gut D are warmer and more melting. The difference on this recording is less conspicuous than it may sometimes be: no doubt because Menuhin himself has a tone so highly individual that whatever he plays on, it still sounds like Menuhin. But the difference can be heard, and it is very interesting.

George Malcolm used a modern harpsichord not of baroque design nor literally of baroque sound. It was made by Robert Goble; and it was subsequently worked over by Malcolm Russell, who gave it his personal attention even in the studio. This harpsichord has pedals for convenience, but has been adjusted for a tone reasonably (it cannot be altogether) in line with the best late-baroque French instruments. It is excellent of its kind, and the kind is such as is ordinarily available and by some preferred.

In the Purcell violin sonata, I used for the bass part a viola da gamba, long in my possession, by Barak Norman, the finest and most famous of baroque English viol-makers. The top D, the A and the E are of gut; the C is of aluminium-covered gut; the G and the bottom D are of silver-covered gut. This is a stringing which cannot be improved upon (except that some gambas may be a little better with an uncovered gut C; but this is unusual). Covered or plastic top D, A and E strings are always, I think, audibly inferior. Except under unfavourable climatic conditions (where their greater stability may be worth some cost in characteristic sound) they are not to be recommended, since an experienced player of the viol who does not fidget too much with his pegs should normally be able to keep the higher gut strings well in tune, and the lower covered strings are going to need skilled management anyhow.

Except for a few examples intended as control samples, Menuhin used a bow in my possession which is of about the same date as his Stradivarius violin, and of comparable excellence. The material of this bow is snake-wood, a rather heavy wood much favoured for bows at that period. It is delicately fluted to reduce the weight without diminishing the strength. The stick when unscrewed is slightly incurved (as commonly with the best baroque bows), but just perceptibly outcurved (almost straight) when screwed up to its proper playing tension. The length is rather more than the baroque average, having just over twenty-five inches of free hair. The stick is quite straight laterally, amply stiff for strength and springy for elasticity, impeccably balanced and of an even resilience throughout. Actual baroque bows as good as this are rare, of course; but it is becoming much less rare now to encounter modern reproductions which, provided the stick is as it should be, play almost as well. We therefore thought it acceptable to use this baroque bow for our demonstrations here.

The baroque bow which I used with the Barak Norman gamba is less decorative, but the stick is admirable, being a little stouter and stiffer, as the bass instrument requires. The date appears to be about the same. My bow-hold is completely at the nut, not a few inches along the stick as some gambists now teach. Both grips have historical support in pictures and descriptions, and can be used to produce artistically satisfactory results; but the grip at the nut gives a longer effective length of hair, which is advantageous in slow movements; and it also gives somewhat greater command of power, which I believe to be very desirable for an authentically robust interpretation, where required, of baroque music.

2 Everyday problems of baroque string playing

Our need for better style and technique in baroque string playing comes before our need for baroque instruments and bows; and the general qualities of transparent sonority and crisp articulation come before such details as correct trills and appoggiaturas. Yet details do have a cumulative effect; and style itself depends largely on small points of technique. To demonstrate this, it would have been possible to construct a systematic series of text-book examples; but that would have left out of account the musical context which always conditions and should condition the details. We therefore decided to use mostly passages, shorter or longer, from actual pieces of baroque music, on the first side; and on the second side, complete movements or complete works, from which the essentials can be picked up and applied to any number of similarly characteristic contexts in baroque music.

The passages selected, and the movements or works given complete, are from familiar composers, since we are not so much concerned here to demonstrate advanced problems or little-known idioms, however significant and valuable, as we are to help in solving a little better some of those everyday problems which are already being solved well by many good modern fiddlers. But in baroque string playing, it is that little better which can make all the difference.

RECORD EXAMPLE I

Example I is concerned with the most fundamental everyday problem for baroque string playing: the kinds of string sound which are required in baroque music, together with the kinds of bow stroke needed for the purpose.

1a is a familiar passage from the first movement of the Brahms Violin Concerto. The bow stroke required is of full length, high speed and strong pressure, taken fairly near the bridge. This is big music; the solo violin is surrounded by a big orchestra; and without this kind of fine bravura assertiveness and massive energy, the piece would go for nothing.

1b is a no less familiar passage from the third movement of J. S. Bach's B minor sonata for violin and harpsichord, played with the same massive energy; but here the result is to overweight the music and denature it. The violinist doth protest too much, methinks. In its own way, this too is big music; but it is a chamber music way, and baroque chamber music at that. It has its own witty sort of assertiveness; but the heavier the tone, the less the wit. The stroke required is not full length, but at most a half-stroke, taken just above the middle; the bow speed should be moderate; the pressure well into the string, but crisp rather than massive, still fairly near the bridge. The good result of this crisper stroke is heard at 1c.

Similar considerations arise in baroque slow movements. 1d is a very nineteenth-century passage from the Gypsy Airs (*Zigeunerweisen*, Op. 20) of Sarasate, played with a spun tone of all that thickly opaque intensity which such music not only justifies but demands. 1e shows the disastrous result of misapplying this sort of thick intensity to J. S. Bach, in the slow second movement of his D minor Double Concerto. Yet if we take out all the passion from the tone, all the vibrato from the colouring, all the intensity from the line, we fall into an opposite extreme which is just as disastrous. This is purity carried to a fault, and we can hear at 1f how weak it sounds. There is, however, a different kind of intensity, not thick, but glowing, which has the necessary baroque transparency and inwardness, as may be heard beautifully at 1g. The stroke is slower, the vibrato is narrower, but the focus of the line could not be keener, and the tone is spun to the finest tension. The baroque bow was used, but modern stringing.

1h shows the same passage, played in the same (right) style, but using gut strings on the Guanerius violin in addition to the baroque bow. The difference is solely in the colouring. It is not very conspicuous, since Menuhin sets his individual colouring on whatever he plays, but it is very attractive. Gut strings may appeal very much to some players (they do to me) and they bring us nearer to the baroque colourings. On the other hand, they do not condition the style, and they are therefore not essential to good baroque performances.

RECORD EXAMPLE 2

Example 2 is concerned with the contribution of the left hand to colouring and to phrasing.

Vibrato is the main consideration here. For colouring the tone, it should ordinarily be used, but in moderation. Most but not all notes require some vibrato, without which there is no life and sparkle to the tone of string instruments: this moderate vibrato can be heard throughout the recording. A few notes may be given a conspicuous vibrato, such as would have been regarded by baroque players as an ornament, and like any other ornament, only to be used for a particular expressive effect: this conspicuous vibrato can be heard in a recitative-like passage from the third movement of Handel's A major violin sonata, Op. I, No. 3, at 2a.

Another consideration, affecting both colouring and phrasing, is position. The lower positions, up to the third, give a clearer colouring and are generally to be preferred in most baroque music; much of the work is best done virtually in the first position. 2b shows a somewhat extreme though quite agreeable fingering up the A string to the sixth position, in the third movement of

Handel's violin sonata in D major, Op. I, No. 13; the rather veiled tone decreases rather than increases the poetry of this essentially simple melody. 2c shows the cleaner and more incisive effect of staying down on the E string, not avoiding open strings. 2d shows the exaggerated colourings produced by going up the G string in the fifth variation of Bach's famous Chaconne in D minor from his Partita II for unaccompanied violin: impressive to the unsophisticated, but not growing genuinely out of the implications of the music. 2e is the same passage fingered across the strings so as to bring out the phrase-divisions by each change of colouring, and is better because it does grow out of the implications of the music, as well as having an altogether more natural sound. But 2f demonstrates in a very showy and difficult passage from Locatelli's *L'Arte del Violino*, Op. III, that the baroque virtuosi were not afraid of exceedingly high positions (up to an almost impossible fourteenth position) when the mood was on them.

RECORD EXAMPLE 2
2*b-c*, Handel, D maj. violin sonata, Op. I. No. 13, 3rd movt.

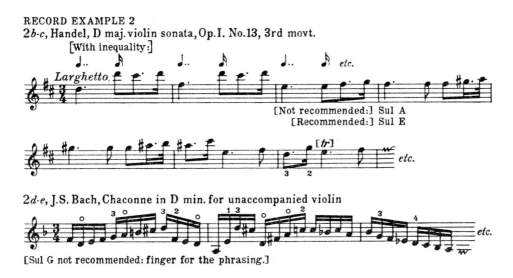

2*d-e*, J.S. Bach, Chaconne in D min. for unaccompanied violin

[Sul G not recommended: finger for the phrasing.]

RECORD EXAMPLE 3

Example 3a shows a small but favourite dynamic effect, the messa di voce, by which a long note increases from soft to loud and decreases to soft again. It is only for occasional use, but 3b shows a suitable case in the third movement of J. S. Bach's B minor violin and harpsichord sonata. Notice also the very clear and expressive phrasing of the paired notes. But the phrase starts in the right hand of the harpsichord with an up-beat group of three notes, not two notes; and it there continues with leaping pairs, not with stepwise pairs. It would therefore be extremely unsuitable and unmusicianly to make the pairs unequal in performance, as a moment's experiment will confirm.

3c, from the second movement of Handel's D major violin sonata, Op. I,

No. 13, shows the type of accentuation, not massive but incisive, which is most typical for baroque music in general. It is done by a moderate finger-pressure on the stick of the bow, released just as the bow starts to move, and where necessary reinforced by a momentary access of bow-speed. In varying degrees of strength this biting accent, sharp without violence, is of the greatest utility, and it will be heard very frequently throughout these recordings. Notice also the very moderate degree of staccato which gives the short notes sufficient separation, without breaking the onward flow of the melody; and by contrast, the smoothness of the cantilena so soon as the longer notes of the sequential suspensions allow an opportunity for it.

3d, from the Rigaudon of the fourth of Couperin's *Concerts royaux* in E, shows the extreme piquancy which is typical for this sort of French movement in particular, where an Italian allegro (as shown in the Corelli recorded on the other side) might require a robuster kind of fieriness, produced by holding on to the stroke a little more solidly.

RECORD EXAMPLE 4

Example 4 concerns the importance of not taking fast tempos too fast or slow tempos too slow.

4a, from the fourth movement of Bach's E major violin and harpsichord sonata, shows too fast a tempo, and too agitated a stroke, there being simply no time to put in any proper phrasing. This kind of false brilliance is not actually implied by the music, but superimposed with most unmusical effect: a temptation to be firmly avoided. The modern bow was used.

4b shows the tempo needed for making a proper phrasing, thereby sounding not only more noble, but more truly brilliant, because it is possible to put so much more into the music. The stroke is a sprung détaché, reposeful and relaxed yet of strong character and ample tension. The baroque bow was used.

In the studio, Menuhin experimented with both bows for this movement. He suggested that the modern bow encourages (though of course it does not impose) a faster tempo, because the vertical elasticity of its incurved stick is narrower and tends to rebound in less time. But the baroque bow encourages (though again it does not impose) a more moderate tempo, because the vertical elasticity of its outcurved stick is wider and tends to take a little more time on the rebound. The baroque bow does make some things easier in baroque music. But in order to show that the modern bow can be got to do what is required, with a little more care and attention, 4c is the same passage, at the same tempo, and with the same stroke, but using the modern bow. It sounds very good.

4d, from the third movement (Larghetto) of Handel's D major violin sonata, Op. I, No. 13, is taken just too slow to have a natural flow, so that to shape the phrases gracefully becomes rather a strain, and even so, the effect is on the sluggish side. 4e is the same passage taken only a very little faster, but just enough to have a forward impetus, and not to hang heavy on the hands. It might with advantage move on slightly quicker than this. The phrasing, when there is enough forward movement, should almost seem to shape itself.

RECORD EXAMPLE 5

Example 5 is concerned with the baroque flexibility of rhythm. What is punctual by the clock is commonly too soon to be punctual by the heart. The stretching of the tempo within the phrase, and the spacing by extending the tempo between the phrases, are of paramount importance throughout baroque music, and nothing so makes a baroque allegro monotonous as bringing everything mechanically to time. Slow movements are less often made to suffer in this way, but the result is just as disastrous when they are. The flexibility of the rhythm and of the tempo is one of the chief features which make these recordings expressive in the proper baroque manner.

This much flexibility will arise from good musicianship alone, provided that the free and joyful spirit of baroque music is well understood. But in addition, there were at the time certain conventions of rhythmic alteration

RECORD EXAMPLE 5
5a Handel, violin sonata in D major, 1st movt., Affetuoso

As notated:

As it may be performed with lilting underdotting:

5b Bach, Fourth Brandenburg, 2nd movt., Andante
As notated:

As it may be performed with optional inequality:

5c Handel, D major violin sonata, 4th movt., Allegro

etc.

etc. (overdotting)

5*d-e* J.S. Bach, E major violin and harpsichord sonata, 4th movt., Allegro

5*e*, literal is best:

5*d*, this inequality NOT recommended:

5*f* J.S. Bach, C minor violin and harpsichord sonata, 4th movt.

which since became forgotten, and which have to be reconstructed in order to get many passages of baroque music more nearly as they were meant to sound; and this will not arise from good musicianship alone, but requires a knowledge of the conventions, the most necessary working rules for which will be found in Ch. XIII above. A few specific cases are demonstrated in Example 5.

5a, from the first movement (Affettuoso) of Handel's D major violin sonata, Op. I, No. 13, is notated in simple four/four, with dotted notes. By the convention of underdotting, this dotted rhythm may be softened off to a lilting, triplet-like flow which approximates to a compound measure in twenty-four/sixteen, and which can, near enough, be notated as such if so desired. 5b, on the other hand, from the second movement (Andante) of J. S. Bach's Fourth Brandenburg Concerto, is notated in simple three/four, with even notes equally notated. By the convention of inequality, these equally notated notes may be livened up to just the same lilting, triplet-like flow, approximating in this case to a compound nine/eight, and, near enough, able to be notated as such. Thus a similar effect is reached from different directions in the notation: in the one instance by reducing dotted notes, approximately to triplets; in the other instance, by expanding even notes, likewise approximately to triplets. The description seems more complicated than the practice: a baroque performer would fall into it from mere grace and habit, and we can teach ourselves to do the same. It is, however, very important not to do it out of context.

5c, from the fourth movement of Handel's D major violin sonata, Op. I, No. 13, is notated with dotted figures, which may be crispened up to a march-like vigour by the convention of overdotting, approximately as if double-dotted (and, near enough, able to be notated as such if so desired).

5d, from the fourth movement of J. S. Bach's E major violin and harpsichord sonata, is notated with triplets for the violin, and even notes in the bass which can be thus tripletized to match; but then notice how awkwardly they tangle with the quadruplet rhythm soon appearing in the right hand (and later, on the violin). 5e shows how much better it is in this instance to take the notation as written, and not with inequality.

5f from the third movement of J. S. Bach's C minor violin and harpsichord sonata, is notated with dotted notes for the violin, triplets for the right hand of the harpsichord, and equal notes for the left hand; but in performance here, the violin tripletizes (by underdotting) in order to assimilate with the right-hand triplets. This is correct, but sounds a little too mechanical because it is done with too nearly mathematical an accuracy. 5g shows the same assimilation done with true musicianly flexibility; and here, the equal notes of the bass, in the left hand, are also tripletized (by inequality) in order to assimilate with the prevailing triplet rhythm. The effect is then very good indeed. Notice also the tripletized rhythm of the long appoggiatura introduced on the last note of the violin's phrase: it is both correct and beautiful.

RECORD EXAMPLES 6–8

Examples 6–8 illustrate some basic ornaments, such as an experienced performer of baroque music may wish to add whether any sign for them occurs in the notation or not.

Some examples of badly performed trills are shown at 6a (where the trill is started wrongly on its lower note); 6b (where the trill is started wrongly

RECORD EXAMPLE 6
Bad trills

RECORD EXAMPLE 7
Good trills

RECORD EXAMPLE 8
Half trills

Mordents

Compound ornament– double cadence

J.S. Bach, *Matthew Passion*,'Erbarme dich', slide and trill:

Donington, sample cadenza for end of Purcell Chaconne

before the beat); 6c (where the turned ending which terminates the trill is separated wrongly from the trill itself); 6d (where the little note of anticipation which terminates the trill is taken wrongly, i.e. long and heavy, as it may be notated, instead of late and light as intended); 6e (where the trill is left wrongly without any termination).

Some examples of well performed trills are shown at 7a and 7b (correctly accented upper-note starts, on the beat, and with smoothly turned terminations); 7c and 7d (also correctly accented upper-note starts, on the beat, but with late and light terminal notes of anticipation); 7e (the literal interpretation as notated), and 7f (the correct trill as implied).

8a shows half-trills (correctly with their accented, upper-note starts, on the beat) in a passage descending by step, where they are particularly recommended. 8b shows mordents (correctly with their accented, main-note start, on the beat, and with their repercussion below their main-note) in a passage ascending by step, where they are particularly recommended.

8c shows a very frequent cadential formula; and then shows it with a correctly performed double cadence, which is an ornamentation admirably suited to it in a great variety of contexts.

8d, from the violin obbligato to the aria 'Erbarme dich' in J. S. Bach's *St. Matthew Passion*, shows a well performed slide in its standard baroque position (correctly accented on the beat), followed by a correctly performed trill (of which the notation as here by an appoggiatura sign is uncommon, but known).

8e, from the edition by Robert Donington and Walter Emery of the G minor Chaconne in Purcell's *Ten Sonatas in Four Parts* (trio sonatas), shows a sample cadenza as it may be added to taste by the performer. This is a fairly long and elaborate example for its baroque context, and many performers may prefer something shorter and simpler. On the other hand, there are many surviving baroque examples which are longer and more elaborate. As so often in baroque music, the options within the boundaries of the style are quite wide, although they would exclude anything approaching the extent and complexity of a cadenza from the classical and romantic periods. The difference is that a baroque cadenza does not have any structural function, but is merely part of that general liberty for free ornamentation which all baroque convention permitted or encouraged.

Our chief demonstration of free ornamentation here will be found in the Corelli solo violin sonata on the other side of the recording, where the specimens shown are probably by Corelli himself and certainly by some baroque contemporary. In the Purcell solo violin sonata, I have provided similar free ornamentation for the slow movements, where it is particularly needed, and must be added by the editor or the performer if the composer, in the usual baroque manner, has not provided it himself. J. S. Bach nearly always did so; but in that, he was exceptional.

3 The complete recordings

The complete recordings bring up in a natural setting many such everyday problems of style and technique, and they also demonstrate how a performance well matched to the implications of the music may shape up as a whole. The overall quality of the line is more important than any separate detail, which ultimately can only be right or wrong in relation to its context. The smoothest cantilena has to be divided into those lucid patterns by which the line becomes intelligible; and the sharpest articulation has to be moulded so that it adds up to a line and not merely to a succession of isolated notes. Menuhin's line makes credible to me that remarkable tribute voiced by a contemporary eyewitness in 1709 (see p. 74 above), that he had 'never met with any man that suffered his passions to hurry him away so much whilst he was playing on the violin as the famous Arcangelo Corelli'. Certainly the passion is balanced, as it has to be for good baroque style, with an underlying serenity and poise. Nevertheless, there is this impetuousness, and it should be there.

There is a corresponding impetuousness in George Malcolm's realizations of the harpsichord accompaniments, improvised by him in actual performance over the continuo bass line (figured bass) which is alone provided by the composer. There are as many legitimate options in continuo realization as there are in free ornamentation; and a performer who prefers his own taste and follows it comes much nearer to the baroque spirit than one who accepts uncritically what is put in front of him. To keep within the boundaries of the style, we have to come up with material which relates musically to the given material; which does not get in the way of the soloist, either by being unrelated or just by being too much; yet which has the interest and variety to give the soloist not only enough sonorous support, but enough musical support. An uninspired accompaniment cannot musically support an inspired composition. Better dull than distracting, no doubt; but a certain felicity in this exacting art is a wonderful asset to the performance.

RECORD EXAMPLE 9

Example 9 is Corelli's D major violin sonata, Op. V, No. 1. In the first movement, slow passages marked Grave alternate with quick passages marked Allegro. There exists an edition printed by Roger at Amsterdam around 1710, and subsequently pirated by Walsh at London, which gives these slow passages, and slow movements elsewhere, in two versions, one set above the other. The plain version (as alone normally given) is in uneventful long notes, structural to the progressions, and never in the least intended to be played as such, although that is what modern performers habitually do. The ornamental version (as here added) has been confirmed as probably though not certainly Corelli's own: if not his, it must nevertheless represent the kind of version which he had been heard to play. And that would in all probability never have been twice quite the same. In performance, the structural notes should stand out firmly as strong pillars supporting the harmony; the ornamental notes *should hang lightly in between*, as passing notes not necessarily involved in the harmony. The cantilena, however, is always sustained, except at breaks in the phrasing, where a marked separation, and often a moment of stolen time, is needed to keep the pattern clear. Notice the emphatic leaning on appoggiaturas and on the upper-note starts of trills. The stroke is well into the string and not very fast; but it becomes a much faster sprung détaché in the allegro passages. The tone throughout is ringing, sweet and never forced. We have good examples here of what is meant by transparent sonority and incisive articulation.

RECORD EXAMPLE 9
Corelli, D major violin sonata Op.V, No.1, 1st movt.
As ordinarily printed and performed:

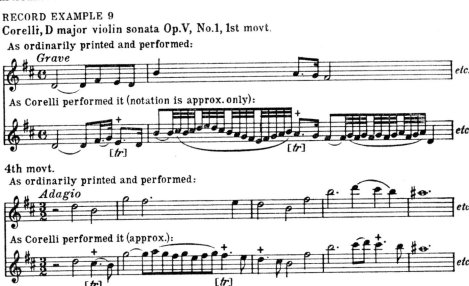

4th movt.
As ordinarily printed and performed:

As Corelli performed it (approx.):

The second movement is a vigorous fugue, with double-stopping on the violin, sounding very robust, but not agitated because the stroke, though firm, is relaxed. The big arpeggios are slowed down a little, so that they do sound big, and not merely too slick and easy. The full chords come on the beat, but are allowed to spread from there sufficiently for them not to sound harsh and ruthless. There are ritardandos for flexibility; and where a chance for cantilena occurs, the most is made of it for the sake of contrast.

The continuously rapid notes of the third movement are very distinctly phrased, and are given plenty of irregular agogic accents (minute prolongations), so as not to sound mechanical. The fourth movement has free ornamentation like the first, and is again a test of finely spun cantilena, decisively broken at the phrase-endings. The fifth movement is a lighter fugue, but it nevertheless needs a solid though sharp stroke, in no way tenuous or trivial.

RECORD EXAMPLE 10

Example 10 is Purcell's only violin sonata (not a trio sonata, as it is speculatively transcribed in the Purcell Society Edition, Vol. XXXI); and I am still indebted

RECORD EXAMPLE 10

Purcell, violin sonata, 1st movt.

to my lessons on this piece from Arnold Dolmetsch fifty years ago, and to the fine performances by his gifted son, Carl Dolmetsch, though the version as here used is my responsibility. It includes free ornamentation, rhythmic modifications, and a harpsichord realization of mine which George Malcolm has greatly improved, and with his usual inventiveness, in course of performance.

The first movement (Adagio) is notated in plain notes and equal rhythms, but performed with increasing ornamentation and some lilting inequality. Notice the melodic character and phrasing of the bass part, and also the transparent sound of violin, gamba and harpsichord in combination, the gamba being preferred to the cello at this time in England. The second movement runs on from the first, with an implied trill on the main theme and an editorial cadenza before the end; the stroke is a light staccato for the eighth notes and a slightly sprung détaché for the sixteenth notes.

The third movement is much improved by the lilting inequality given in performance to its equally notated rhythm, and by some very considerable and requisite free ornamentation, which is lightly played so as not to conceal the basic melody. The fourth movement again runs on, its piquant vivacity brought out by a stroke quite short and crisp; but the tempo must be no faster than this, since there is a hint of poignancy beneath the sparkling surface, very typical of this most English of baroque composers.

RECORD EXAMPLE 11

Example 11 is the Forlane from the fourth of Couperin's *Concerts royaux* or collection of pieces in the keys of E minor and E major. It has an elegance just as French as the poignancy of Purcell is English; but here, too, we need a tempo sufficiently moderate to bring out the depth of feeling beneath the surface charm. The sub-title *gayement* is to be taken rather as a mood-word than as a time-word; for the music tells us that it is gayness of that Shakespearian ripeness from which tears are not far away. The rondo theme is especially melting, and needs the same quiet dynamic and warm colouring each time it returns. The episodes invite contrast of tone and tempo, especially the section in the minor, here given a dramatic retarding and accelerating for which there is sufficient historical evidence in the baroque authorities. But quietness takes over again with the returning theme. We could end with no fitter demonstration of Couperin as 'more pleased with what moves me than with what astonishes me' (see p. 72); and altogether of that romantic emotion which so often glows beneath the classical orderliness of baroque music.

Reading List

Bach, Carl Philipp Emanuel. *Versuch über die wahre Art das Clavier zu spielen* [Essay on the true art of playing the keyboard], Berlin, 1753. Pt. II, Berlin, 1762. Facs. Leipzig, 1957. Engl. trans. as *Essay on the True Art of Playing Keyboard Instruments*, W. J. Mitchell, New York, 1949. [Pt. I, generally important; Pt. II mainly for accompaniment]

Boyden, David D. *The History of Violin Playing from Its Origins to 1761*, London, 1965 [Indispensable]

Corelli, Arcangelo. *Sonate a violino* [Sonatas for the violin], Op. V, Amsterdam, [?1715]. Ed. Joachim-Chrysander [1890]. [With 'the ornaments . . . composed by Mr A. Corelli as he plays them']

Donington, Robert. *The Interpretation of Early Music*, New Version, London, 1974. [Long and detailed]
A Performer's Guide to Baroque Music, London, 1973. [Compact]

Geminiani, Francesco. *The Art of Playing on the Violin*, London, [1751]. Facs., introd. D. Boyden, London, [1952]. [Valuable baroque text-book]

Menuhin, Yehudi. *Violin: Six Lessons with Yehudi Menuhin*, London, 1971. [Fundamental]

Mozart, J. G. Leopold. *Versuch einer gründlichen Violinschule* [Essay in a thorough Violin-School], Augsburg, 1756. Facs. Vienna, 1922, Frankfurt am Main, 1956, of 3rd ed., Leipzig, 1956, and Leipzig, 1968. Engl. trans. as *A Treatise on the Fundamental Principles of Violin Playing*, E. Knocker, London, 1948, 2nd ed., 1951. [An important text-book for virtuosi]

Purcell, Henry. *Ten Sonatas in Four Parts*, London, 1697. Sonatas VI (Chaconne) and IX, ed. Robert Donington and Walter Emery, London, 1959. [With editorial ornamentation, etc.]

Quantz, Johann Joachim. *Versuch einer Anweisung die Flöte traversiere zu spielen* [Essay in an instruction-book on playing the transverse flute], Berlin, 1752. Facs. of 3rd ed. (Breslau, 1789), Kassel, 1953. Engl. trans. as *On Playing the Flute*. E. R. Reilly, London, 1966. [Actually an all-round guide to late baroque musicianship]

Index